AF426664

Return to the Source
Volume 2

Talks by
Sri Mahaprabu

Copyright

Copyright © 2024 Sri Mahaprabu

All rights reserved. No part of this book may be reproduced or used in any manner without the prior written permission of the copyright owner, except for the use of brief quotations in a book review.

To request permissions, contact the publisher at www.srimahaprabu.org

BHAGAVAN RAMANA MAHARSHI

SRI MAHAPRABU

Table of Contents

Note from the Recorder

This book is a continuation from the first volume published in 2023. Below is the background about the book, reproduced from the first volume.

This book has the power to transform your life. Not just by its content, but by your coming in touch with the Master from whose lips these words of Wisdom have been spoken. Sri Mahaprabu is an enlightened Master from Tiruvannamalai, India who has been quietly guiding a small group of sincere seekers for over 17 years.

Before meeting Sri Mahaprabu in 2019, I was searching to fill a deep void that was eating into an otherwise very successful position in life. I was the founder & CEO for a US based technology company for over 15 years and was serving the community at various levels. Still, this feeling of incompleteness, combined with a deep thirst to fill it, continued to possess me. I spent a few years immersing myself in Vedantic study along with reading the works of great Masters from across the world. And yet I found that despite all the book knowledge, deep down I was completely in the dark as to who I really am. Making matters worse, I could sense how all this accumulated knowledge was only strengthening my ego. This took the suffering to another level.

It was sheer grace and a miraculous set of circumstances that found me at the feet of Sri Mahaprabu one evening at his house. That day my life changed forever. I began to see firsthand how an Enlightened One lives in this world. An embodiment of Love and Intelligence, flowing moment to moment in harmony, in total Surrender, with things happening around him in perfection. While his message was exactly that of all the great Sages, the way he communicated it so I could understand its deep import, and the divine presence from which those words were uttered, began to resonate with me deeply. After innumerable Satsang sessions with him, my doubts, misconceptions and misunderstandings began to evaporate. And in their place blossomed a clarity I had never had before. It took a long time to come out of the effects of the knowledge overload I had accumulated. Then, after sitting for long sessions with him, listening to his deep insights, followed by hours of silence in his presence, I began to get in touch with a never-before-experienced feeling which was both within me and without. Something of an indescribable quality that shined in bright contrast to the turmoil and ugliness that has been tormenting me inside for years.

By grace, the thought occurred to me early on to record our conversations with his permission. I did it for my own help. Those precious words should not fall through the cracks of my memory. I would listen to them again and again. Later came the thought that I should share this invaluable treasure with other seekers like me. I approached Sri Mahaprabu who readily agreed and in his characteristic way said "Let it happen. IT will decide when." Almost two years later, for the first time now, his talks are being made aware to the world in the form of this book. The first in a series we hope to bring out.

These talks cover all the essential topics including: Our Fundamental Problem, Why we suffer, All about the Mind, Body and Soul, How to deal with Worry, Fear, Anger, Desire, How to transcend the ego, Realize our True Self, and Experience Eternal Freedom.

The best part about all these talks is that they do not require any special knowledge or background on the part of the reader to understand and imbibe the message, since they simply beautifully kindle the presence of THAT which is already within each of us. Sri Mahaprabu is a Master at bringing it out and putting us in touch with the Truth.

How to use this book

Please read the introduction to Sri Mahaprabu and his Journey, followed by the first couple of talks. After that, there is no prescribed order to follow. Please go to whatever topic that could be of help to you at that moment.

It is my sincere prayer that you find this book as a stepping stone to the real solution that ends all your suffering – Coming under the auspices of a living enlightened Master like Sri Mahaprabu.

Sincerely

Satchitanandam
Disciple of Sri Mahaprabu

Sri Mahaprabu

Introduction

Sri Mahaprabu is a *Brahma Jnāni*, who attained liberation in the year 2003 by the grace of Bhagavan Ramana Maharshi. Since 2006 he has been conducting *satsang* regularly near Tiruvannamalai. The following is a brief introduction to Sri Mahaprabu.

Venkatesan (birth name of Sri Mahaprabu) was born into a very ordinary family in southern Tamil Nadu. It wasn't until he was in his teen years that a very strong desire began to consume the youth. The desire to know about birth, death and who he really was. Seeing death all around him at a young age and realizing the certainty of his own death strengthened this desire into an unstoppable urge, one that must have been simmering and evolving for many lives past. This single-pointedness brought him to Tiruvannamalai in the year 1993.

Entering Ramanasramam for the first time, he saw the board which described Sri Bhagavan's death experience in detail. He instantly knew he had come to the right place where all his questions would be answered. Being a sincere devotee of Lord Annamalaiyar (Shiva) and Sri Bhagavan Ramana Maharshi, it was by sheer grace that he was soon connected with Sri Annamalai Swami Ashram in Pelakottu (adjacent to Sri Ramanasramam). He would go there regularly to attend the various *parayanas* being conducted, as well as for the monthly Swathi Puja of Sri Annamalai Swami.

He used to spend most of his time in meditation at the forests of Arunachala hill, Bhagavan Sri Ramana's *samādhi* and Sri Annamalai Swami's *samādhi* shrine. He diligently pursued the path of self-enquiry taught by Sri Bhagavan and Sri Annamalai Swami. Thus, for 10 years he underwent a rigorous *sādhana*, unwavering in his determination despite numerous trials and tribulations, thanks to his burning desire to know the Truth, his steadfast *bhakti* (devotion) and his strong faith in Bhagavan. And on January 1st, 2003 **'IT'** happened. The dissolution of the individual into the universal. Sri Mahaprabu was born.

For the next forty days, he was mostly in a state of blissful *samādhi* going into indescribable depths of experience. The next three years were spent mostly in solitude, revelling in a state that words cannot describe. Not only did his spiritual friends observe a significant change in his lifestyle but were able to feel a tremendous silence in his presence. They began to share their questions with him and received an inner clarity they had never experienced before.

In 2006, Sri Mahaprabu received a divine message from Lord Buddha who instructed him to share his experiences and guide true seekers of the Truth. With the blessings of Sri Buddha, Mahaprabu started his *satsangs* in Paliappatu (a small village at the outskirts of Tiruvannamalai) in 2006. Devotees of Annamalai Swami including Sri Sundaram Swami who was the caretaker and disciple of Annamalai Swami for 21 years, began to attend these *satsangs*. Sri Annamalai Swami, before his *Maha-samādhi* in 1995, had told Sundaram Swami that another living enlightened master will come to guide him towards enlightenment. Sundaram Swami and other trustees were able to recognise Sri Mahaprabu, as the living enlightened master that Sri Annamalai Swami had predicted and have been continuing their spiritual *sādhana* under the guidance of Sri Mahaprabu till date.

Various seekers of the Truth from different parts of Tamil Nadu and abroad started attending *satsang* with Sri Mahaprabu. Among them, Sri Mahaprabu began to guide only those seekers who are sincere, dedicated and truly committed to realising the Truth in this very birth. His *satsangs* and meditation camps are happening regularly in Paliapattu, Tiruvannamalai.

Satsang

Being in *satsang* with Sri Mahaprabu is like simultaneously diving to the deepest depths of *jnāna* and soaring to the highest peaks of *bhakti*, shepherded throughout by a sweet and fragrant power that is none other than Love.

Since it is the Supreme Power that speaks and acts through that bodily frame, **there are no traditional rules, methods, techniques, not even scheduled timings. Yet *satsang* happens as sure as day follows night and night, day.**

During *satsang*, hours can pass by like minutes, as we join him in meditation, or melting to his devotional singing, or listening to the words of great *jnānis* (Bhagavan Ramana Maharshi, Annamalai Swami, Ramakrishna Paramahamsa, Adi Sankaracharya, Buddha, Osho, Sadhu Om, Avudaya Akkal, Vallalar Swamigal, Bharathiyar and Thayumanavar to name a few) or just sitting spellbound by the words of wisdom that flow so beautifully and spontaneously from Sri Mahaprabu's lips. Words that shatter all preconceived notions, **resulting in a clarity that no book or teacher can ever come close to giving.** Only a *Brahma jnāni* like Mahaprabu can.

No question goes unanswered. And yet he reminds us that it is the questioner that needs to disappear. "Meditation is always happening," he says. "It is the one who wants to meditate, that needs to dissolve. **The Experience being sought is already there and is not something to be attained. It happens only when 'you' are not there to experience it.**" *Satsang* with Mahaprabu is undoubtedly the greatest, best-kept secret, not just in Tiruvannamalai but in this entire world.

Perfection

Just being in Sri Mahaprabu's presence and observing how he carries himself, gives you a glimpse into what perfection is. **Every movement, every gesture, every word comes from a point of total calm, total presence, without the slightest agitation whatsoever; whether he is in the market or in *satsang*.**

Next to him, our actions stand in stark contrast; hurried on the outside, spurred by the turbulence inside. And he knows it. Nothing escapes his watchfulness, even though he is not looking at you. "With Awareness, With Awareness" are the words you will hear him say so often.

Unique approach

A look back at history reveals how the Supreme Power manifests itself as *Brahma jnānis* in different eras; each of them so different in their post-enlightenment life as it were. Some stay silent, some serve as a beacon to those who come, while others become a light that spreads far and wide.

Sri Mahaprabu's uniqueness is this: Once he embraces a sincere seeker, **he comes down to his or her level, working tirelessly with the seeker, day after day, at every step in the journey.** And he even says as much, that "ensuring the disciple attains *jnāna* in this very life, is all that I work for." Such is the boundless love and compassion that he IS.

Sri Mahaprabu continuously **creates situations for the disciple** to serve and to be in *satsang* with him. It is this combination of *satsang* and *seva*, classroom-learning and real-world practice, in close contact with the Guru that weakens the grip of the ego over time. And after continuous, repeated erosion, it finally surrenders. "Only when you have totally surrendered, can the Truth even enter", says Mahaprabu.

Bhagavan Ramana Maharshi once said, "A disciple in the hands of a Guru, is like prey caught in the mouth of a tiger. There is no escape possible." **That Tiger is Sri Mahaprabu.**

Sri Mahaprabu's Journey

Sri Mahaprabu attributes his enlightenment entirely to Sri Bhagavan Ramana Maharshi. **"Adhu Bhagavan potta pichai" (that is the alms that Bhagavan gave this beggar)** he often says.

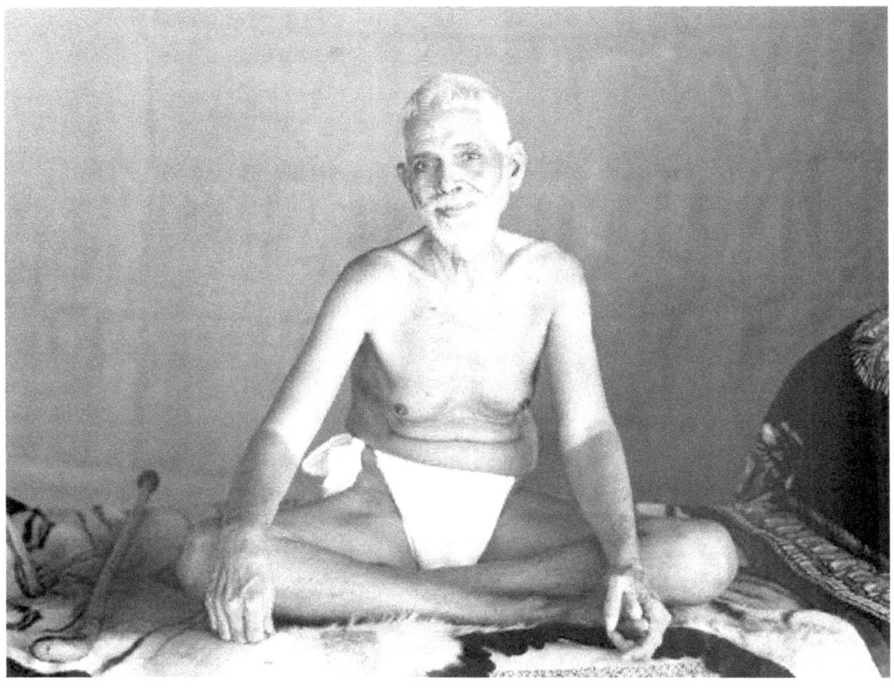

This picture of Bhagavan is framed in Sri Sadhu Om Hall, where Sri Mahaprabu conducts Satsang.

THIS IS THE JOURNEY OF A YOUNG BOY FROM A SMALL VILLAGE IN TAMIL NADU WHO WOULD BECOME CONSUMED BY THE QUESTION 'WHO AM I' AND PURSUED IT TILL THE END, RESULTING IN HIS AWAKENING.

THE CONTENT BELOW IS RECORDED ENTIRELY FROM SATSANGS WITH MAHAPRABU DURING THOSE OCCASIONS WHEN HE WOULD RECOLLECT THE PAST. THESE ARE HIS WORDS, ADDRESSED BY HIM IN 3rd or 1st PERSON.

Childhood

Venkatesan (birth name of Sri Mahaprabu) was born on 11th July, 1974 in Namakkal, Tamil Nadu (his maternal home) and grew up in Pudhuamma Palayam, Perambalur District, near Trichy. He came from a typical conservative, middle-class family. His schooling from 2nd grade through 12th, was in nearby Thurayoor. He was the eldest child, with a sister and brother.

When Mahaprabu recalls his childhood, the one thing that stands out was his loving nature, a loving heart for all things and beings, especially human beings. His love was such that he would touch a leaf and embrace it, pray to any mountain he saw and shed tears at the sight of any suffering. He was especially loving to his parents, who were no less than God for him. At nights out of sheer love and gratitude, he would massage his mother's feet till she asked him to stop. His father kept a distance and wouldn't encourage it, so the boy would wait till his father slept and then massage his feet. He was especially close to his grandfather, who was a very quiet and hard-working man who largely kept to himself. He too was very fond of the boy. Sri Mahaprabu remembers a song that his grandfather used to sing to him often. *Ulagalam unarndhu vodhuvadharku ariyavam...* Years later, when Sri Mahaprabu entered the big temple at Tiruvannamalai for the very first time, imagine his surprise when he saw this song inscribed on the temple walls. He took it as a very good sign.

From young, he was inclined to only speak the Truth, even if he knew it would cause harm in certain situations. He was also highly energetic and cheerful, always on the move and was never one to waste any time. His loving nature combined with this high energy propelled him to help others a lot. He would help as much as he could at home and outside. In school he always excelled in academics, thanks to a sharp focus he had which kept him very attentive in class. At home he would daily recollect and assimilate what was taught. This was enough. He did not have to study much for exams and yet would top his class. This continued all the way to high school where he earned several accolades in education and extra-curricular activities.

The Jolt of Death

When he was 12 years old, his dear grandfather died. Seeing death for the first time, especially the death of one who was so dear to him had a deep impact on the child. He saw the anguish of those around the body, how it was taken from the house and cremated. So many questions began to torment him: Can he hear us crying? Where will he go now? He went to the burial ground and was the last one to leave. While there, he was almost mad and at the same time was observing things with the objective mind of a scientist. Won't this happen to me? It is going to happen for sure. This was the first time he sensed these kinds of questions in him about life. **This event was the main reason why he turned to Jnāna.**

He also had an inner fear of death. He feared for the death of his parents, his brother and sister, his own death. As fate would have it, he would soon witness so much death around him. His grandmother committed suicide a few years later. A close friend and classmate of his died in an accident. The entire body was burnt. Mahaprabu himself took the body to the hospital for the post-mortem and then to the burial ground and cremated him. His *virakthi* (frustration) was at its peak. When is my time to die? I was speechless for 3 days. All your education, skill, money will all go to mud. Born as a fool, you will die as a fool. This kept pricking me so painfully. Soon another close friend of his would die by drowning in a lake nearby. Mahaprabu remembers the incident clearly. He saw a crowd at the lake and asked what happened. He remembers immediately taking off his shirt and diving into the deep waters to save him. But alas, he could only retrieve the dead body. All this had a tremendous impact on the young mind. The questions about life and death became stronger and more compelling.

Pharmacy College - A turning point

After completing his schooling with honours (he not only topped his class but also was one of the toppers in the entire district), in 1991 he joined a two-year program at a college of Pharmacy, where he began to learn about the human body and medicine. A point to be noted here is that Mahaprabu had no interest in pharmacy or the life-sciences. His academic interests were in Engineering and his top scores would have easily gotten him admission to any college of his choice. Yet his father intervened and insisted that he become a doctor. Mahaprabu tried protesting, telling him that he was not interested, nor did he have the required scores in those subjects to get admission into medical college. His father wouldn't budge. To not displease him further, the young lad gave in. As he did not get admission into medical college, he had to settle for a 2-year course in Pharmacy. Why this is so relevant is that at the time of his graduation from high school, there was no engineering college in Tiruvannamalai. Only after 2 years would it be built and commence. How beautifully nature has guided the boy, making him wait

2 years, just so he could come to study in Tiruvannamalai, the *Jnana Bhoomi* – Land of Enlightenment.

An important phase of his pharmacy education was the training program before graduation. He was assigned to the post-mortem unit of a big hospital. The 90 days that followed, would change him forever. Day in and day out he witnessed so much death. Bodies would come and pile up. Many were accident or suicide victims. He was asked to do post-mortems on them. Slicing open bodies, hands drenched in blood, he would remove organs such as the intestines, heart, brain and examine them. This happened on a daily basis. Soon he lost all sense of normalcy. Daily he would wake up, go to work sitting in the bus like one who is possessed, put in long hours working in such a horrifying environment and return home, only to go back the next day. He was like a zombie.

On the one hand he saw the world racing forward with people entertaining hope and enjoyment, while death kept coming unannounced and unmercifully through accidents, crimes and natural causes. **He was shaken to the core of his being.**

After graduating, he spent a few months working in various nearby villages that did not have access to doctors or medical help. He soon realized the inability of modern medicines to cure diseases. Added to that, he saw their harmful side effects. This created a serious conflict in him. One of ethics. He could not accept such a profession for the rest of his life. So he made a strong decision to change career paths. With great difficulty, he convinced his father that he would pursue an Engineering degree.

Coming to Tiruvannamalai

One evening as he was laying on his bed in a state of total despair, not knowing who he was and no one to help, he had this vision. It was over-powering. He saw in a flash, several births of his. Where he was living with different parents and different siblings in each birth. It happened so fast, yet so clearly was it seen. He was shocked beyond belief. He realized that this is how each birth was being passed. Totally believing that he was an individual as told by his parents, that he had a family, he lived with them, for them, but only to die and take on a totally different body and different parents without any regard whatsoever for his previous father and mother. At that moment he lost all his attachment towards his parents, siblings, possessions and life itself. He decided to leave. He could not stay with them a day longer. Remember, this was the boy who would die for his parents.

The very next day he received a telegram from the engineering college in Tiruvannamalai confirming his admission. He saw this as a glimmer of hope and thanked the Supreme Power.

As mentioned earlier, fate would ensure that Tiruvannamalai saw its first engineering college open that very year as though it was built just for Mahaprabu to come to Tiruvannamalai. He got admission there and soon found himself on a bus heading to a place known for its great jnanis (jnana bhoomi) but without the slightest notion about it, or about Jnana. Yet there was this unmistakable deep thirst in him to know who he really was.

For the next 10 years, he would be consumed with finding the answers to those questions that reverberated in him stronger and stronger. Who Am I. Where did I come from? How did I enter this mother's womb? When I die what will happen? Will I enter another womb? Then what is the purpose of this life attached to these parents, if I am going to repeat it all over again with another family? My entire foundation was destroyed. How many lives I would have lived and died and married and died, different relations, so many fears, jealousies, anger, revenges. And yet I could feel a love deep inside me. I wondered why it doesn't come out. I decided that whatever happens, I will find out who I am.

Engineering College

The 4 years from 1993–1997 was simply a way to get away from home and be in solitude while searching for the answers to life's questions that consumed me. Even though I was a student who topped his class and had aspirations for a successful career when young, now things had changed entirely. I had no interest whatsoever in a commercial path. I used to think: All that I need is a small room to stay, 2 times a day food for this small stomach, 2 shirts, 2 dhotis and 2 towels. Imagine, this was my attitude at the age of 19!

As soon as I reached Tiruvannamalai I heard about a jnani named Yogi Ram Surat Kumar. I remember people saying that meeting a Jnani was a good thing for seekers. I had a *darshan* of him. Then I saw the entrance to Sri Ramanashramam. I went in. There was a board there that described the death experience that Bhagavan had as a young boy, and how he left home to come to Tiruvannamalai. That gave me hope that I had finally come to the right place too, Tiruvannamalai. I prayed to Bhagavan sincerely, but beyond that there was no connection.

As I started my studies, the inner frustration continued. I felt the entire world was empty and life was meaningless. All are going to die but they are ignoring that totally with not even a mosquito bite of a sensation, they are all living as though they are permanent. Totally dejected and desperate, I decided to go to the famous Siva Temple in Tiruvannamalai. I remember going in through the North entrance. This was the first time I was entering the temple. There I saw many verses were inscribed on the walls. But there was this verse right in front of me. I read it:

Jnana tabodanarai va endru azaikum malai Annamalai.
Annamalai is the mountain that welcomes seekers of Jnana.

Suddenly, all the energy that I had lost in 3 years, flowed through the body in a rush. It felt like it was 1 Lakh watts of electricity. Though the mind created this feeling, it was a huge tonic for me. A huge boost. I decided to focus on this exclusively from now on.

But in my 2nd year, I faced setbacks in the form of health. An accident in the gym hurt affected my right hand for a long time. That same year I developed an illness that made me bed-ridden for 15 days. I couldn't even get up. It was as though I was paralyzed. A fever would come and go. As a result of all this, my studies began to take a hit. And then tragedy struck again the next year. Another close friend was involved in an accident. I rushed him to Chennai and admitted him in a hospital. Fortunately, the boy would survive. I returned the very next day to Tiruvannamalai to write my final exam. I remember sitting in the examination hall, shirt full of blood stains. I failed that exam. More failures would follow. The arrears (failed subjects) piled up. There were 14 of them I had to clear. Despite all the frustrations I knew that I had to successfully complete the degree. It was a matter of survival. I began to study hard and take up the arrear exams in addition to my current semester exams. I remember sitting in those examination halls like a dead body. Only the hand would move while writing the exam. There was no enthusiasm at all. I felt like I was possessed. Total frustration. I was doing it just to complete the cycle. A dead body taking up the pen to write something. That was how it happened. And yet I passed all his exams, unbelievably clearing all 14 arrears alongside. I could now graduate.

Finding a Job

As graduation neared, Mahaprabu wondered what he was going to do. I had almost become mad. One thing is for sure. One day this body will go. Before that I need to find out Who I am. **I will not leave Tiruvannamalai till I find out. Even if this body dies it is OK.** I just wanted minimum money for one meal a day and a place to stay in Tiruvannamalai. Friends in college were applying for jobs in big cities and abroad. Many of them left. I had no interest in all that. I approached the owner of the hotel where I would eat daily. I begged him for a job in the hotel where food and boarding would be provided with a minimal salary. He was shocked that I was serious but didn't think it was appropriate for me to take up such a job given my education. As a last resort I was even to live on the street and beg for food so I could stay in Tiruvannamalai and continue my practice.

I finally turned to Lord Siva (Annamalai Temple) with extreme devotion. I sat there crying and begged. "Please do not make me leave Tiruvannamalai without knowing who I am. Keep me here even as a beggar, but please don't send me away." At that time a friend of mine happened to come to the temple. Seeing the tears on my face, he said 'Come with me. I will take you to someone who can help you.' I was then introduced to Thiruvadithuli Swami. A great *bhakta* (devotee of Lord Panduranga). Even though he did not conduct *satsang* or answer Mahaprabu's deep questions, I found a joy in serving him. For nearly 5 years I served Thiruvadithuli Swami continuously. I remember helping wherever possible. Be it in the kitchen or cleaning all the toilets regularly, especially on crowded days.

Miraculously (just like how an engineering college was opened in Tiruvannamalai the very year that Mahaprabu was looking for admission) a private polytechnic college was inaugurated in Tiruvannamalai, and he was offered a job as a lecturer there. Now he was assured that he could stay in Tiruvannamalai and pursue his *sadhana*. Nothing else was more important. His gratitude towards the Supreme Power became stronger and stronger.

And from that year 1997 onwards, something began to pull him inside to just sit. **He did not know it was meditation back then, but it kept pulling him to sit.** So many times, whenever there was a chance, he would sit quietly. After graduation when everyone left the hostel, he stayed alone in that big building (he was the hostel warden too) for 45 days. Most of that time was spent sitting silently. Soon he was at a stage where he could not avoid sitting.

His *seva* to Thiruvadithuli Swami continued till 2002. In those 5 years, he would visit Ramanashramam mainly because Thiruvadithuli Swami conducted *satsang* in the nearby Annamalai Swami Ashram.

Marriage

For someone who was so single-pointed about knowing the Truth, and who lived his life like a total renunciate, it is surprising that the thought of marriage would enter his life. This is how Mahaprabu recalls it happening.

During the engineering college years from 1993-1997, while coming by bus from his town to Tiruvannamalai, he would usually sleep. But each and every time, he would automatically wake up at a particular place called Ulundurpet, when the bus passed by the temple built for Sri Ramakrishna Paramahamsa. He felt a strong connection to Sri Paramahamsa. He decided to visit the temple. It was January 1st. He went in and sat in the hall with other devotees but in total silence inside. A Swami was coming by, blessing each devotee by touching their head. Just as his turn was coming, Mahaprabu remembers a single thought that consumed him: I want to attain *Jnana* in this very birth itself. At that moment the Swami blessed him. Mahaprabu later found out that it was the celebrated 'Kalpataru Day' in remembrance of the day when Sri Paramahamsa blessed everyone under the Kalpataru tree at the Cosipore garden house.

Mahaprabu continued: It then happened that year when I was sitting in meditation for a long time, Sri Ramakrishna Paramahamsa appeared to Mahaprabu and told the following: "You will get married. Children will be born. If you go against it, it will still happen. You cannot stop it, so don't fight it. Don't worry about it. But it will not be an obstacle for you. Just live like a *bhakta*."

At that time Mahaprabu had the least interest in women, marriage or even the idea of marriage. But he respected the words of this great saint and let things happen. And it happened exactly as predicted, in the year 2000.

Sadhana

I had made it very clear to my family that *sadhana* was my main priority in life. Other than my wife and son I had dropped all other family connections a long time ago. Even my parents. My love for them was still the same. I would call them once every 3 months and enquire. But no visits, no matter what the occasion. There was tremendous pressure from all sides. 'Why are you not coming to the wedding? Why aren't you doing this for us? Why are you always sitting in *dhyanam*?' So much opposition I had to deal with, at home and from outside. But as my understanding was very clear, my decision was firm. I knew these were all not real. **But I still did not know who I was. That was unbearable. I had to find out.** The determination was very strong.

Once I felt the peace inside, I was always naturally drawn towards sitting and going deep within. I stayed away from books and external guides. People would often say 'This book is great; you should read it. You can take it.' My reply was 'Please, if you want to see me again, don't raise this topic again.

What I need is already inside here. I know it is not out there. I have gone inside. You also please go inside.'

Every day I would wake up at 4 AM and sit in *dhyanam*. At 5:30 I would pick up a friend on my moped and go to the forest. He would sit at a certain spot. I would go further inside and sit. We would be there till 8 AM. Then I would come home and get ready to leave for work. At the college, I told all the staff that I will only speak during class hours. That I was paid to do that. Outside class if anyone wanted to speak to me, I would kindly request them to please write it on a paper and I will reply in writing. I would urge them to please help me in my practice by agreeing to this. In the college, I would meditate whenever I had time. To avoid being seen, I would go to the library and sit behind the end of the shelves. In the lab, I would sit behind heavy machinery. On returning home, I would wash and almost immediately leave to that same spot in the forest, sit there for over an hour and return around 7 pm. Then I would take the wife and son to Ramanashramam. On the way I would get them some snacks. They would sit at the entrance. I would sit in Bhagavan's *Samadhi*. This was a daily routine.

Bhagavan Ramana

To me Bhagavan was everything. He was my father. It was exactly like a son living with his father and coming to see him in his room. I saw the room where I lived and the ashram as part of the same house in Tiruvannamalai. I would speak to Bhagavan from the heart. 'How are you father? I am doing well.' It was a very deep and affectionate connection. I would sit there till 9:30 PM till they asked me to leave.

I would then ask the family if they wanted to eat something and get them what they wanted. Straight we would head to the Girivalam path where it splits from the main road. Wife and son would sit near some trees, a bit away from me. I would sit there in total stillness. Till 11 pm I will be there. They would never call me or disturb me. This was my daily routine.

On Sundays, as there was no college, I would make the most of it. After getting whatever was needed for the home, I would leave for Virupaksha cave around 9:30 AM. I would pack some date fruits and water. This was my lunch. Sitting in the cave I would tell myself strongly: O Mind. You have everything you need for the rest of the day. No work is there for you. Snacks are also here. The only allowance for the body is to go to the toilet. With this determination I would sit in Virupaksha cave for hours together. Around lunch time I would eat the dates, drink the water and again sit. Only in the evening around 5:30 or 6 PM, I would get up. The whole body used to tremble with hunger. I would come down the steps and go to a tea shop, have a tea to get some energy and go home. This was the routine every Sunday.

2002 - The Crucial Year

The year 2002 was when Venkatesan had no choice but to leave Thiruvadithuli Swami. He had dedicated 5 years to serving him but found himself no closer to finding the Truth about himself. And no help was coming from the Swami. He remembers that day at the Mettur bus stand waiting for the bus to Tiruvannamalai. He knew he would never go back to Thiruvadithuli Swami. Five precious years had gone by and yet he found himself nowhere closer to the answers he was seeking. I felt totally lost and abandoned. Did not know where I was going in my spiritual *sadhana*. There was this extreme desire to know the Truth but there was no proper guidance at all. No Guru who could hold his hand and take him. Frustration was at its peak. I began to physically collapse. I almost felt like I was going to die in that bus stand. I could feel my heartbeat slowing down. It was like a heart attack coming. It was with these thoughts that I nearly collapsed. I simply laid down flat on the bench there.

It was then that the voice of Bhagavan Ramana Maharshi came to me loud and clear. "I am here for you. Why don't you try me one time?" This gave me the energy to get up and somehow reach Tiruvannamalai.

I went straight to Ramanashramam and prostrated to Bhagavan. **There the same voice came again and instructed me to read the book 'Ramana Vazhi' by Sri Sadhu Om.**

I read the book and I read it one time only. Instantly I was able to see where all I had made mistakes in the past 5 years. All my *sadhana* had been rooted in the idea of a person. I had accepted that this person existed. That was the mistake. I decided that going forward I will never give room to the idea of a person. It was Sadhu Om that gave me life again. Without him, there would be no Mahaprabu.

Mahaprabu enhanced his meditation much more. He was mostly alone or in the forest by the Girivalam road.

The point is that this much strong *Vairagya* came from the previous *janma*. Not this birth. Without even a living Guru to help him, he was able to progress. Mahaprabu did come across many teachers, but always could see that he was ahead of where they were. He had gone very deep. The only thing he was missing was the actual experience. Only the match had to be struck for the fire to catch on.

So Mahaprabu analyzed his mind deeply. He found only two issues. Fear and Worry. Fear was always about the future. Yet I cannot change the future. Worry always stemmed from the past. Yet I cannot change the past. These 2 drag me down all the time as if I were tied to two big rocks. So Mahaprabu made a very strong decision. I should not think of the past or future anymore. Only stay in the present. For 1-year Mahaprabu was only in the present moment. At that time a friend gave him a xerox copy of a book "Power of Now" by Eckhart Tolle. Mahaprabu did not read it, only saw the cover. After a year, Mahaprabu understood that with effort you can control the mind. But how long can you do this? The minute I stop the effort, Fear and Worry will return. I am still not free.

For one year it was a very strict practice. That year all illnesses stopped. No headache, fever, stomach pain, typhoid etc. People used to say there is a lot of *tejas* (brightness) in you. '

But life was not smooth even then. There were a lot of critical moments. His child died during delivery, one month premature. At 4 a.m. he got the news, and yet from 4:30 to 6 a.m. he still did his meditation. He arranged for money. Did all his paper corrections at the college by putting aside all thoughts. Finally in the evening he reached and moved his wife to a private hospital, took the baby to the burial ground at 9 p.m. Dug a hole and buried his first child. All with complete awareness. His close friend was with him throughout. He would become a disciple later.

When thoughts came, he just ignored them. Stay in the present. The mind won't go anywhere. This became a habit. The mind found joy in the present moment. While he was teaching class at college too, for the entire hour he would be in the present moment, while teaching. Something from the back penetrates and comes out through the mouth. Always fresh. A dynamic Stillness. After completing the full hour of teaching while being in the present moment, he would look out the window and see the Arunachala Hill. Tears would flow down his face.

And in the evening, no matter what, from 8 to 9 p.m. I was always in front of Bhagavan Ramana's Samadhi at Ramanashramam. Soon *Resagam* (expiration of breath) and *Kumbakam* (retention) happened one day. Then there was a flash: Breathing is not happening, but living is going on. The lungs keep a residual supply of air. Oxygen goes in slowly and carbon dioxide out slowly. At that point he felt every cell vibrating. It was tremendous. And then he sat watching the mountain without a single thought, except the consciousness of wanting to be in the present moment. Even that wish or will disappeared. There was a happening. *Brahmikka Thakkagara.* (Very powerful) A flash came and went. Back to the present moment.

The Previous Evening

On December 31st evening, (2002) Mahaprabu was sitting with two friends at the tea stall outside Ramanashramam. His friend told Mahaprabu, 'When I sit next to you my mind turns off by itself.' What? Mahaprabu asked, making sure he was aware in the present moment. This was a longtime friend, especially during all these *sadhana* years.

This friend then told the other friend about Karl Renz, an enlightened soul who was visiting Ramanashram and would conduct *satsangs* when he felt like. He was a free soul. Not many could understand him. A great artist and musician. He even mentioned that this Karl Renz did not accept Eckhart Tolle's Power of Now as a teaching. This caught Mahaprabu's attention. As his friend was talking, this Karl Renz was coming towards them! His friend told Mahaprabu, 'There he is!'. Karl looked like a very ordinary man with his shirt untucked. As if by impulse Mahaprabu rose and walked towards Karl and shook his hand. The friend introduced them. Karl said, "Come for *satsang* tomorrow, 10 to 11 AM"

At the time Mahaprabu was in complete surrender to the Supreme Power and had unshakable faith in IT, as IT has given us the earth, air and body, so IT alone is in control. He replied, 'If IT permits, I will come.' There was no hesitation, liking or disliking. His friend later said he spoke like a co-*Jnani*.

Enlightenment

The next day at 9:30 it came to Mahaprabu's awareness that Karlji (Mahaprabu always addresses him with the suffix *ji* for respect) had invited him for *satsang* at 10 AM. The place was across Ramanashramam. Downstairs was a mess (food serving place). Upstairs was an open room with just a thatched roof where the *satsang* was held. Mahaprabu had 100 Rs left of his salary. Using that, he bought flowers, fruit, biscuits and arrived there.

There was only one spot left, that too in the last row. About 20 feet away from Karlji. Mahaprabu didn't look at Karlji's face. Just sat with closed eyes without missing the present moment. Even to get here, while leaving, starting his bike, climbing the steps, sitting, throughout he was always in the present moment. Nobody can imagine how sincere the practice was. 100% sincere.

Mahaprabu was just sitting, in full alertness of present moment. Inside there was a tremendous silence. Karlji was talking to a lady to his right. "You just simply drop your mind". These words somehow reached Mahaprabu who was not even in the line of hearing, even though there were numerous people talking. Mahaprabu recollected that as he was totally attentive in the present moment, those words reached his ears despite him being so far away.

On hearing those words "You just simply drop your mind", a laughter took place deep in the belly. Like a bubble forming deep under water, and on its way to the surface. It was developing into a powerful laugh, but it came out as a smile. Mahaprabu's thought was that this: "The whole problem is the very mind itself. He is saying 'Simply drop the mind'. How can you simply drop it! Sounds unrealistic."

Then came the words from Karl, as if he had read Mahaprabu's mind. "Come on, ask the question!" (He probably saw the smile on my face)
Mahaprabu: "Myself?"
Karl: "Yes! You."
Mahaprabu: "You are telling 'Drop the mind.' But how to drop the mind?"
(Mahaprabu had not spoken much English in 6 years).

Karl: "First you check whether there is a mind to drop."

The match was struck

Mahaprabu checked. I am here. I can feel the body, feel the world, feel my own existence but I am unable to feel the existence of the mind. Ah! It hit him. Beyond words came an understanding, that all this time I have been worrying about something that doesn't exist. I had created an entity called the mind and then tried to control it. Because of the present moment practice for 1 full year his mind always had just one thought, that is to stay in the present moment. For one year, just one thought. As one paper cannot be called a book, one thought cannot be called a Mind. Mahaprabu skipped the present moment thought and became attention. **I searched deeply but could not find a trace of a mind. That was it. Then like something faster than light, I went inward. No mind! But I am there! Going deeper but I am still there. Before it was in flashes. Now it was continuous. I could stay with it. Joy, Bliss. I lost total awareness of surroundings, crowds etc. I merged into the universe. The thirst that started at 19, was quenched.**

Two hours passed. Opened eyes. Karlji hugged me, embraced me and said, "You are good". The friend who had come with me had left long ago. From then on for the next 40 days, daily 10 am to 12 noon, Mahaprabu would go there to Karlji's *satsang* and sit on the steps, just out of love for him and be immersed in deep *samadhi*. He did this for 40 days. For this he took off from work, using up all his casual leave (type of holiday allowed in India) in half-day chunks plus the Pongal holidays. He remembers a few statements of Karlji that had a deep impact on him: *'Nothing is lost, and Nothing is gained.' 'You cannot Not be yourself.' And 'The light of Shiva is not Shiva.'*

Those 40 days, daily after *satsang* he would go home and spend the next 4 hours again in deep *samadhi*, usually 1 to 5 pm.

Then one day while walking on the Girivalam path, his friend said let's go see Karlji as he was leaving. They met Karlji. He lifted Mahaprabu and dropped him. Mahaprabu also did the same. Karlji, an enlightened soul himself, told Mahaprabu that of hundreds of people, it feels like he came all the way to see Mahaprabu. 'I was not keen on making the trip to India this time, but felt that something was dragging me here. Now I know what it is.'

Mahaprabu would say later: We have to lose the idea that we have a mind. Because Mahaprabu was in total 'No Mind' state for 1 year, he was able to drop. The same words "Simply drop the mind" for a normal person wouldn't have worked, since he assumes the mind exists. For Mahaprabu there was no mind. Mahaprabu compared the stage just prior to this to an umbrella where the strap is removed and ready to be opened. Just the button needed to be pushed, but where the button was, wasn't known.

See the grace of Bhagavan. He decided, 'This boy is OK. It is time.' So, he sent a living *jnani* in the form of Karl Renz to come all the way to Tiruvannamalai in order to free me. See the importance of a living Master. Even though it took only a few minutes of interaction with a living Master, his presence was most important. Without his presence there, I don't know how much longer it would have taken or where I would have ended up. That is why I have tremendous gratitude for Bhagavan.

This picture with Sri Karl Renz was taken in January 2003, just days after the Awakening of Sri Mahaprabu in the Satsang hall near Ramanashramam.

Taken around the same time as the previous photo, Sri Mahaprabu remembers this moment vividly. After 10 years of tremendous struggle and suffering, a smile of unimaginable relief and joy.

The next 3 years

The next three years were spent mostly in solitude, revelling in a state that words cannot describe. He would tell us later: Mahaprabu would go through ever-increasing depths and heights in *samadhi*. He wanted to see the totality to the fullest extent that IT would allow him. And IT took him. Mahaprabu was saturated with bliss and perfectly content leading the quiet life, engaging in only the minimum required with the world.

But in 2006, on the day of Buddha Purnima, that changed. Sri Mahaprabu was in a deep silence when he began to feel very strongly, the presence of Lord Buddha. It was as if a powerful stream of energy from Buddha was entering him from above. He remembers it distinctly. The instruction came to carry the work forward. To help others. Mahaprabu had not known much about Buddha at all until then. Nor did he have any experience with the spiritual teaching. As if hearing him, **the message came from Lord Buddha: "You just go and sit. I will speak."** That was the message.

Satsang

The very next day, Sri Mahaprabu left for Tiruvannamalai. Having lost his individuality there was no plan on his part. IT guided him, just like IT had been doing since that morning in 2003. He reached Paliapattu, a small village 8 Km from Ramanashramam in Tiruvannamalai. Thus, with the blessings of Sri Buddha, Mahaprabu started his *satsangs* there in 2006.

A few seekers of the Truth from different parts of Tamil Nadu started attending *satsang* with Sri Mahaprabu. Among them, Sri Mahaprabu began to guide only those seekers who are sincere, dedicated and truly committed to realising the Truth in this very birth. His *satsangs* and meditation camps are still happening regularly in Paliapattu to date.

Sri Mahaprabu in deep Samadhi one morning at his home in Tirunelveli in 2007

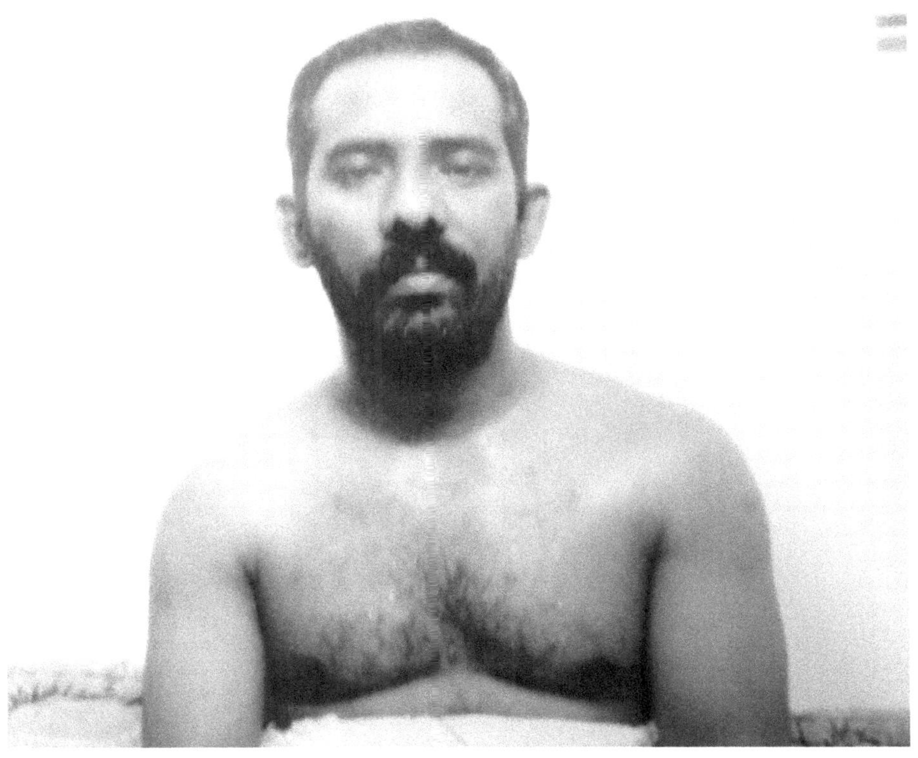

Sri Mahaprabu had just conducted Satsang (on a button-phone), and at the end of Satsang he went into a deep Samadhi. This was in 2009, also in Tirunelveli.

During the month of May 2008, Sri Mahaprabu conducted a 20-day continuous Satsang in Tiruvannamalai. He would give rest to the body for only one to two hours each 24-hour day! One of those mornings, Sri Mahaprabu had just come out of a deep Samadhi and was seated on a chair, when a disciple placed flowers on his shirt and took this photo.

TALKS

Role of a Master

Who is the Master and how the Master helps the Disciple to find out his true nature. Sri Mahaprabu spoke about this at length.

World as a Theatre

Say there is a highly thrilling movie. Take 3 examples of it being watched. One person watches it on his mobile in the palm of his hand. Another watches it on a big TV screen. A third person watches the same movie in a theatre on a giant screen, with full sound effects, etc. Who will be most impacted by the movie? Obviously, the person watching it in the theatre. Why? Because everything is amplified. And you appear so small in front of it. When the movie is in your palm, you are in control. But in the theatre, it is reversed. If that is the case with a pre-recorded, unreal event such as a movie, imagine HOW BIG THE UNIVERSE IS. AND THE EVENTS ARE HAPPENING LIVE, CONTINUOUSLY. How small you feel. How impactful the world can be on you. So be very careful in this world. You will be sucked in.

The Master

The Master cannot use his own brain. There is no 'he' to use it. The Supreme Power uses his brain. He remains in total Surrender. Only when a person has reached this point, is he Enlightened. Everything is operated by the Supreme Power. Reaching this point is Wisdom. So from then on, he will continue to be in Surrender. He will never use his brain himself. Instead, the brain will be used by God, the Supreme Power. This is the fact.

If so, then depending on the Surrender of the disciple, automatically the Supreme Power will work through the Master. So it is not in the hands of a Master to favour a particular disciple. Equally, it is not in the hands of the Master, not to favour a good disciple. Since the Master is not taking the decision. There is no 'he' there which is acting. The Supreme Power is acting. Also, the Master has no likes/dislikes to favour a disciple or not. Nothing will come from him. Everything happens as the Supreme Power intends. The Master cannot change it or stop it. That is the law of Nature. So, have faith in this law. This gives you hope. If you deserve it, whatever is needed for your improvement will come to you. No one can stop it. If you don't deserve it, no one can make it come to you. Therefore it all comes down to you, your sincerity and your effort. As you climb up, it will come to you. See the nature of Surrender. The Master cannot do anything. Otherwise, Bhagavan Ramana Maharshi would have given enlightenment to everyone. The great Buddha could not give enlightenment to his wife or his son easily, nor to his mother who raised him from young.

Where the Master helps

Therefore, the one who is not ready will not get it, and the one who is ready cannot be prevented from getting it. So it comes down to what? Your readiness. There comes the role of the Master. He prepares you for that readiness. He makes you ready. He is the resource through which Godliness acts and gives the instructions to prepare the disciple to make him ready. Once a disciple is ready, no one can stop it. So, readiness is the core. Who can prepare the disciple? The Master. Just like, who can cook well? One who has cooked many times and mastered it. The Supreme Power gives certain individuals the ability to prepare disciples for enlightenment. Only they can prepare. No one else can.

The Disciple's job

So, a day should come in your life when you say 'Gurudeva, hereafter I will not use my brain. I have totally surrendered to you. Whatever you want me to do, tell me. I am here to execute. I will not deviate even a tiny bit.' From that day only you can count your progress. Not before. This alignment is needed. This is preparation. Reducing all your deviations and coming into total alignment with the Master. And when can the Master prepare you? When you have the above commitment 100%: 'I will not use my brain. Whatever you want me to do, I will do.' That day, the real journey starts.

So what is important is the strong interest you have in knowing yourself. Can that strong desire come automatically? No. You have to develop it yourself. It will not come to you.

The danger of disowning your ego.

As you drop the ego, there is a risk of developing an 'I don't care' attitude. It is like this: *A person loves his wife dearly. One day he comes to know that from the next day onwards she is leaving him to go with someone else. From then on, will he have the same care and love for her?* No. Similarly, *a person owns a car. He takes care of it so well. Washes it, polishes it, etc. His neighbour buys that car. And he lets it sit in the driveway. Will he even bother to go and clean it?* No. So, when we own something, the behaviour is different. When we don't own it we behave differently. You become indifferent to that thing. A carelessness sets in. This is natural. The same thing happens in Spirituality. So far you have owned your ego. You have taken care of it so well. But in Satsang, with the continued presence of the Master, you cannot own your ego. You have to drop it. As you start to drop the ownership, you will develop an indifference to life. A 'nothing matters' attitude creeps in. This carelessness, lack of involvement, and insincerity is very destructive. A tough period. But the Master helps by saying, "Now is when you have to be very sincere. Sincerity towards the Truth." A total opposite. Imagine if there was no Master. You will self-destruct. Every seeker of Truth has to cross this critical phase. Because they all have to drop their ego. When they do so, they are likely to become totally indifferent and careless. Actually, this is the point where you need 200% sincerity. It is extremely difficult to do it alone. There comes the help of the Master. At that point you have to become sincere towards the Master. So far you were very sincere about your ego and your life (a false one). But now you should be very sincere to live for the Master. If this transformation happens, where you are now living for the Master and not for you, then you can cross that tough zone. For this shift, you need a lift, from the Master who is God's gift!!

For a simple thing like a wife or a car we lose interest over time. For something that has been 'you', all your life, for so many lives (your ego) when you begin to drop that, imagine how much you will suffer. Only the Guru knows this suffering. He knows that you will experience frustration but that extreme frustration needs to transform into extreme sincerity now. Imagine how difficult. It is like putting your entire life at stake. *It is like you have lost all your immunity and are totally weak and lying down. But you have to take on the most strenuous task.* So, he will prepare you slowly so that you develop the strength. This cannot be rushed. It has to be done extremely cautiously. This preparation can only be done by the Master. Because it is easy to say 'I don't care' and become totally indifferent. But what is needed is that you must be unattached, but responsible. Drop attachment and develop responsibility. It is extremely difficult. Only the Master can help.

24th July, 2021
Rest House at Paliapattu

Acceptance vs. Achievement

The Feeling of Existence is the only original feeling. The true identity. And yet we keep missing it continuously. And we look for it outside, through various Achievements. This short and beautiful talk contrasts the solution - Acceptance, with the problem - Achievement. Sri Mahaprabu had just ridden a bike all the way from Chennai to Tiruvannamalai (since cars were not allowed during the Covid lockdown) in order to be here for Satsang as usual. An amazing feat if you know what Indian roads are like, that too for 200 Km.

The Original Feeling

We can hide our sorrow but we, cannot hide our happiness. ALL Feelings are generated based on identification. Only one feeling doesn't depend on anything. It is the Feeling of Existence (*Unarvu*). That I exist is not an inference, not a perception nor means of knowledge. It is a direct experience. It is the only direct experience. That's why Bhagavan said try to hold on to the Feeling of Existence. All have it. How does a man in a dark room confirm he is there? A dead body cannot confirm this. Existence manifests in living and non-living things, but it can be felt in living beings, especially human beings. That is why the human form is special. That is why we must make use of this extremely rare opportunity of this birth. But at the same time in a human birth, there is a much higher probability of missing this Feeling of Existence. Dogs don't need to worry about dressing well to go out. But even they have an ego. Imagine humans, how much ego they have. So many things we worry about, such as dress, hair, wealth, roles, status, etc. A human birth is like walking on a knife's edge.

The original feeling is the true identity. All other feelings are mind-made. That's why Jnanis don't give importance to the disciple's feelings. That's why Buddha was called *Sunyavadhi*. If someone died, there was no reaction on his face. Someone born, no reaction. Even if the stars said this baby would destroy the world one day. Buddha is a man of real feeling. He always enjoyed the Feeling of Existence. So many kings and beggars existed in front of Buddha. But they were all mere identities. Buddha just Existed. He was so pure. Original existence. No oscillation. That is true Surrender. That's why all Jnanis refer to Buddha.

Acceptance is needed, not Achievement

Worldly success is not possible for all. But enlightenment IS possible. Because it is an Acceptance, not an Achievement. Sadhana, books, Yoga, who asked for all those things? Basic Acceptance we aren't able to do! A child accepts the father as his when the mother says he is your father. The same faith is needed in the Master-Disciple relationship. That Acceptance is needed. Faith is needed. Have faith in my words that you are not a human being. I am not expecting anything from you. Just out of love, I am telling you, if you have faith in my words, remember my words, again and again throughout the day, no matter what you are doing, if you remember this, everything will be alright. This was said by the Master of Nisargadatta Maharaj. Is there any loss for you in remembering this? That's all his Master said. Nisargadatta's Master.

But so many are doing all kinds of things that are just not required. Only do what is required. You do so many things other than what is required. This gap (despite your efforts) makes you feel unfulfilled. Because still you have not done what should be done. Achievement is at the mind level. Acceptance is heart level. Come from mind to heart. Atma is the heart of all.

The other name for Acceptance is Surrender. When you are in Surrender you'll Accept everything. I am talking about Acceptance in a Master-Disciple relationship. Not a general acceptance of everything. This is the only way to attain it. Whoever accepted Buddha, attained. Whoever analyzed Buddha, did not. Acceptance is the end point. Analysis is the beginning and stays there.

Surrender will give you energy (Mahaprabu riding on a bike for 200 Kilometers during the lockdown to Tiruvannamalai for Satsang). Surrender means you aren't giving anything. You are only going to get. Still, people are afraid to Surrender. If you are afraid of giving, you will be afraid of getting also. When the Master says Give, he is preparing you to Get. People who are afraid of Love, never get Love.

Effort is needed to achieve something. No effort is needed to Accept something. Achievement is through performance. But Acceptance only needs a behavioural change. If you want, if you decide, you can. But the decision must be very strong. And for that, you need to come to Satsang. Your head portion is not allowing it. If your head could be removed for an hour and put back, you will Realize what is existing here and now. So, erase everything. The head should be like a clean slate. Only whatever is here will be reflected. Now, you are soaked in various colours (female, male, father, husband, etc). So, you should always have that Awareness that I'm not a human. Meditation is 24 hours.

Keep feeling that Existence in you. In front of that intelligence, your ignorance cannot win. Ignorance can never know Intelligence. So, as you keep feeling that presence in daily life, that intelligence will begin to shine. And whenever ignorance comes in front of you, that intelligence itself will correct it. Over time, the mind will stop. This practice must be done in daily life. Don't entertain the idea that you are in an ashram and are allocating time for Dhyanam when you sit. That is Maya too. Your mind will be quiet then and disturb you at all other times.

August 1st, 2020
Rest House at Paliapattu

Who is doing it all?

This conversation happened as Sri Mahaprabu was on the road, driving. Through the example of driving, he makes us understand a fundamental truth. That for things to happen, the idea of a separate "I" is just not required. A must read!

The *Gavana Shakti* (the power of Attention within us), using the body, hands and legs is driving the car all the while. And it has been doing this, even though there is no thought of a separate 'I' here. IT is moving the hands and legs to navigate the car amidst tremendous traffic. So, there is no need for the thought of "I" as a separate person. The *Gavanam* inside is doing everything carefully. It is aware that the person in front should not be hit, the car must stay on the left, the car should not slow down too much or the car behind will hit this car, etc. Now in all this, is the thought that I am driving the car necessary? Without that thought can't the driving happen?

SC: No. That thought is not needed at all. Even for us, that thought is not needed, but we think it is needed.

Mahaprabu: I'm asking in general. Not you or me. Is that thought needed? Will the car come to a halt in the middle of the road?

SC: No.

Mahaprabu: Correct. Whether I take a decision or not, the *Uyir Shakti* (literally translates to Life Energy) inside is observing all the traffic around, giving the brain instructions as to what to do and is operating the hands and legs through the muscles etc. That *Uyir Shakti* is providing the energy for all this. The question is, do "I" as an individual supply the energy to do all this, or is that energy coming automatically from inside?

SC: The energy is flowing automatically.

Mahaprabu: Yes. The car engine gets energy from fuel. That is limited. The Body's energy comes from food. Does that *Gavana Shakti* need anything for energy? No. If you are hungry, it will show that you are hungry. If you are full, it will show you are full. But does that Attention need any energy to sustain itself or operate?

SC: No.

Mahaprabu: Yes, which means there is no relationship at all between *Gavana Shakti* (Attention) and energy. The energy that the body needs comes from food, water, and air. All three are needed. Not just one of them. All three provide energy to the body. Using that energy and the brain, the *Gavana Shakti* tells the brain don't go there, go here, turn here... If petrol is low, go here. If the body is hungry, it directs the body through the brain, to go there to put food into it. So, this *Gavana Shakti* is doing things beautifully. Whether I am observing this or not, whether I think "I am driving" or not, the system is being operated. So, for this system to operate the car, which is operated by the body, which is operated by the Source, AM "I" NEEDED? (the thought that I am an individual)

SC: Not at all.

Mahaprabu: Exactly. This example is of a very small system, a body operating a vehicle. In the exact same way for the entire Universal system to run, it doesn't need the thought of You and I. Even without that, it will run.

Going deeper

SC: It appears that this notion of individuality that we all carry around is a false and unnecessary layer on top of a self-running system.

Mahaprabu: Yes, but isn't that causing the whole problem here! So, we have to live our life with this understanding at all times. See, the *Gavana Shakti* is always in a 'don't mind' state. If petrol is low or empty it will simply point out and the car will stop. It will not get upset.

SC: Does *Gavana Shakti* know objects? Like a car, petrol?

Mahaprabu: Yes it does. It is for that reason that it created the brain to know these objects. Does the *Gavana Shakti* have a tongue? No. Yet the tongue is used by IT to taste so many things. Let's say there is another Shakti behind the *Gavana Shakti*. Call that Atma. The *Gavana Shakti* is just Observation. You should not think *Gavana Shakti* as God. For now call *Gavana Shakti* as X. It will just present the situation. It does not take decisions. Then who is taking the decision?

SC: Brain.

Mahaprabu: No. Brain is outside the *Gavana Shakti*. If you think Brain is taking the decisions then who made the decision to create the brain! It can't be *Gavana Shakti*. The decision-maker is behind all this!! (Laughing!!). And to make decisions he needs attention attentiveness. So one of the decision maker's attributes or properties is this X, Attention or *Gavana Shakti*. Next, to make any decision a wisdom is needed. Call that wisdom Y. Next, to do anything and everything you need an interest, a love. Call that Z. Behind all this is the Decision Maker. You can call that W.

So, God or Atma is a combination of all these 4: W, X, Y, Z.

With all these, decisions are taken by HIM. The Brain is not taking the decisions. If you think that the Brain is taking these decisions, who has taken the decision to create the brain? (Laughing). So using all this, things are happening. Attention is needed to get information. For this, the Attention needs instruments. So senses were created. Through these senses he collects information, sees it, and operates accordingly. We will talk more about this later. Remember.

Now, back to the car example, the very idea of "I" is not necessary at all. Whether you have the thought that you are a separate person or not, the system of W, X, Y, Z is doing everything and has brought me to the college by turning left, right, stopping at lights, stopping for traffic, etc. So for the whole system to run, the idea of an individual is not at all necessary.

I love you.

Gurudeva.

With the above words, Sri Mahaprabu ended the conversation. I am waiting for the day when he will resume it.

————◆◄◄◆►►◆————

August 2nd, 2021
Driving back to Chennai from Tiruvannamalai

Trying vs. Crying

In this talk Sri Mahaprabu beautifully compares self-effort versus devotion, highlighting the risks and advantages, and recommends a path for seekers.

Recall your life. Have you not made any mistakes knowingly? Have you not hidden so many mistakes of yours from others? For all these things there will definitely be consequences. Even after coming into the so-called Spiritual Path now that we know all are God's creations, we still for example have anger in us, tremendous anger. As we have anger in us we can do bad things easily. We are ready to fire back at so many people. We are like barbarians even in this birth. Now go back to just a few births. Imagine all the mistakes you might have made. To release us from all these mistakes, the Supreme Power has to shower its Grace. We have to become eligible for that Grace.

Without His Grace, we cannot even put effort. If you ask for His Grace, he will not give it immediately. He will look at your list. Based on that he decides whether Grace can be given or not. So, to bring His grace even after seeing the list, the only way is to Cry. 'O God, knowingly or unknowingly I have done so many things.' If you are unsuccessful in your efforts such as meditation, it shows that you are unable to put in the required effort, which in turn shows that you are not getting that much Grace to put in that effort. And why aren't you getting that much Grace? Because your list is huge. Now you cannot demand God. You have to beg, cry, 'Please release me; please forgive me.' Only by crying, crying, crying will his heart melt. He will at least take your file from the shelf and leave it on the table. He will wait. After a while, he will look in your direction. Is there a crying sound coming or not? Only when your crying sound pierces his heart, only when you are at the edge of do or die, when your attitude is 'If you do not give me your Grace I will die', only then will he open your file and sign – 'Ok. Excused, Release him!' Once he shows Grace, everything will happen.

Do you know the effect of His grace? His Grace is such that without putting in any effort you will attain Enlightenment. At that time alone you will realize that it was NOT your effort, but it was always His Grace. That is why all Jnanis sing His praise. Then what is the meaning of effort? That is for your ego. It believes in effort. But we have no choice but to begin with the ego. If you don't see progress, remind yourself that the effort is not enough because Grace hasn't showered. The control switch is in His hand. You have done so many sins knowingly, and you are asking for Godliness. How is it possible? You should deserve Grace. We should demolish the hard rock-like structure you have built over births. How? By crying for forgiveness. Beg, "O Lord I know I have sinned, but I have a tremendous desire for Godliness. I want to live with you alone. I need you alone. Do whatever you want to do to me, punish me, but give me a place on your feet." This should be your state. Then the doors of Grace will open.

Actually, what you want to realize, and feel is the flow of Godliness and Grace. That flow is available like a ductless gland. Similarly, there is a ductless connection with God. But the 'i' in you, hard like a rock is a block to that flow. And that makes you very uncomfortable and suffer.

Surrender

That is why I recommend Surrender. When you are in total Surrender you know that nothing is in your hands, then you cannot have your own ideas, your likes and dislikes, your own plans. So, practicing Surrender is needed. As and when things happen, good or bad you will hand it over to God. This will bring Godliness into you more and more. This is the way to break the chain of thoughts that have hardened like a rock. It takes tremendous strength to break that rock. To go from here (the notion of i) to There (Godliness) is very difficult. The 'i' will not let you move there. Your own mental make-up will prevent you. To break it, we need tremendous strength. A very easy way to gain that strength is Devotion. But as your Devotion increases, you will see that these are rocks of ice, and they will melt quickly. When you Cry in devotion, that strength will come to you. The more you Cry, the strength will come like a heavy flood. Any rocks will be melted.

That is why even Jnanis cry for Grace. The great Advaitin, Bhagavan Ramana Maharshi says in his composition Aksharamanamalai: *Like a magnet and iron filing attracted to it, please do not separate me from you O Arunachala.* And *If you do not reach me O Arunachala, I will melt like water and die crying.* These are the words of Bhagavan Ramana. No one highlights them. Everyone talks about Self-Enquiry when they mention Bhagavan. Bhagavan used to read Bhagavad Gita and would cry. Why? Out of devotion. These incidents are all recorded. The great Advaitin.

Trying vs. Crying – Effort vs. Devotion

In today's world, it is not that hard to make a comfortable living to meet all your basic needs as a Person. This leads to inertia, which will prevent you from going inside. Where is the incentive? What is the need? You will live and die as a Person, somewhat comfortably.

With self-effort when you will taste the peace, the silence, is a big question. Through devotion, in each and every moment you will be in peace.

In devotion, there is no chance for you to miss the path. But with self-effort, you are likely to miss the path again and again.

In self-effort, 'you' are going to do it, and as 'you' are responsible, victory and defeat are in your hands. The ego in you will choose between the two, and be comfortable. But in devotion, you will not choose. You will beg, cry, and even demand victory.

In self-effort, darshan (the vision, experience) is not guaranteed. After a point, you will leave it easily and continue to live a normal life. Because the decision to continue or drop is with you! You will be cheated easily. But in devotion, you will not give up that easily. You will be frustrated but as you know that it is all in God's hand you will keep praying and asking Him.

For self-effort to succeed, it takes a type of strong person with a good character. But devotion is open to all. Even the worst sinners have become the greatest devotees and Jnanis.

Self-effort in day-to-day situations is very difficult to remember and practice. But devotion is very easy to practice in day-to-day situations. It is very easy to Love God. *For example, imagine a boy in love. No matter where he is, he can think about her and be lost in her. Before going to bed, immediately on waking, when he sees someone like her etc.* The same can be done with God, who created all this which we see, including us.

A beautiful example

It is like this: *You are on the steps. You have to reach the top. You can either Try or Cry. By Trying to climb the steps, there is a lot of risk. You might fall back at any time. Also, you don't know how many steps there are.* Your mind has to put tremendous effort to keep climbing. *But when you totally Surrender to God, forgetting yourself totally, when you Cry for His Grace, hearing you He will come down the steps to you.* What better way is there? And even if he doesn't come, as you have surrendered to His Will, and you know that He exists for sure, you will wait. You will cry. He then gives you the strength. One day or the other his Grace will shower upon you.

Actually, you are not. He is behind you. It belongs to Him. Is there any difficulty in surrendering all His belongings to Him? The 'i' that is binding you is the disease. The very problem you are trying to solve is this 'i'. It is a very strong and worst disease. You have to forget yourself. In self-effort, 'you' the 'i' putting in the effort will be there continuously.

But just by thinking of God, who created everything that we see, including ourselves, you can forget yourself. That is why Ramakrishna Paramahamsa said that he who sheds tears just by hearing the name of God is the best devotee and is qualified for enlightenment. It is possible to develop that kind of devotion. We should make this possible in us. That is the only way you can forget yourself. And that alone is needed.

April 16th, 2022
Rest House at Paliapattu

How it Works

A Jnani describes the play of the Supreme. Sri Mahaprabu went into a good degree of detail as to how the play happens. The inner workings. How it works. Why it works that way. The role of the Faith. And as always, he ends with what must be done by the disciple. Once again, the time was way past midnight. He was driving (or better stated: driving was happening)

As far as the body is concerned what are its main needs? Food and some care. Just as a hired driver of the car (not the owner) takes care of the car. He takes care but not like an owner would. At the end of the day the driver goes home without any sense of possession. Like that, without a possessor or possession, a basic maintenance of the body should go on.

Body is an object. Similarly with all objects, the same type of relationship is needed. A possession-less, minimal care.

When it comes to us (seekers), we should live only for 1 thing. *Anma Anubavam* (Experiencing the Atma). And what is that *Anma Anubavam?* We have to be very clear. It is already in us. Not anywhere else or with anyone else. And the day when that *anubavam*, experience happens, it is going to happen only in us. Therefore, there is no question whether I will attain it or not; he has attained it; I have not; etc. Because it is already in us. All those types of thoughts are madness. But for a new seeker, we don't say it is madness to have those thoughts. Because he wouldn't take the next step then. For him, we should congratulate him, encourage and motivate him. For a mature seeker, you have to drop those types of thoughts as they are a hindrance. Attaining *Atma*, becoming enlightened, all these are meaningless words. Throw them away. We know there is a living entity, that is conscious, knowing (*Arivu*) and is loving, full of love (*Anbu*); and that living entity is what we are. In addition to it, there is an entity of flesh and bone. For the flesh and bone, we take minimum care, as it will die one day. We don't need to bother about it much. Your thighs cannot know. Your hair cannot love.

The inner-workings – Knowing and Love

SC: What do you mean by *Arivu?* Is it Intelligence?

Mahaprabu: Not exactly. Intelligence is something that comes from experience. *Arivu* is more an ability to know; an ability to think and an ability to take decisions; an ability to perform. Whether the thoughts, decisions and actions are right or wrong comes later. But ALL living beings have these faculties: Knowing, Thinking, Performing. Even an ant. It knows whether the sugar is there or not. It knows whether it wants it or not. It knows to act based on this information. This entity of *Arivu* (Knowing) + *Anbu* (Love) is in ALL living beings, in addition to some physical component: i.e. flesh, bones, etc., depending on the type of animal. This physical component cannot know, cannot think, and cannot perform. ONLY IN THE PRESENCE OF THAT ENLIVENING ENTITY, this physical entity appears to function.

So, call the physical component, Part A: The Body (dead body). Part B is a Being which can know, which can think, which can perform. And through various experiences, it develops intelligence. Because, what you call intelligence is really used for knowing in a better way, thinking in a better way and performing in a better way. So put that aside. What is in-built is these two things, Part A and Part B. And within Part B, there is one more in-built ingredient: Love, *Anbu*.

The whole purpose of the body and the ability to know, think and perform, is what? It is to share and enjoy the Love that is already in it. This Love is in-built in B. It wants to enjoy its own Love. Take any life. They all want to enjoy this. The Ribhu Gita says this about an enlightened being: *'Thannileye thaanaga thanitthu nindru, thannil inbam pusippavane jivan muktan.'* – Abiding in himself, he enjoys the bliss of his own Self.

And what is happiness? It is a symptom. Where does it arise from? From Love. For example, *When a man hugs a woman, he actually feels the love in him. Sharing that love gives him joy. He is not sharing the joy which then gives him love (laughing!!)* It might appear that love is coming from joy but when you look closely, it is love that brings joy and not joy that brings love. When do you feel happiness? Whenever the love that is in-built in Part B flourishes, blossoms and comes out. For example, *In the atmosphere is there air or not? There is. Are you happy when it is there just as air, or when it blows as a breeze? You are happy when it is a breeze. But the air was always there! You should have felt joy. You did not, until it blossomed as a breeze.* So, in order for happiness to be felt, it needs the love to blossom. That blossoming, that flowing of love is what is felt as happiness.

The play of Atma

Part A has a temporary existence. Part B does not, and it takes many Part A's. When Part B decides to take a body (Part A), it will take one.

SC: I understand. But then how do you explain the fact that Atma creates experiences that don't result in the feeling of Love? For example, so many sad things are happening.

Mahaprabu: It does not want to create those experiences. In order to enjoy the love that is in-built, it uses the knowing-thinking-performing to create experiences. On the way to enjoying the love, when the knowing, thinking, and performing does not happen correctly, it leads to so-called adverse situations. Unknowingly it ends up in sad situations. Do people enjoy sadness all the time? No. They all try to come out of sadness. Who is that 'they'? The same Part B! It wants to come out of sadness. How? Again through knowing, thinking and performing. Intelligence is thus growing! Part B then reaches the right track after the sadness is gone. And after several such experiences, one day it eventually returns to Godliness.

Sadness is not its goal. It is a milestone on the journey. See, this is the whole play. It is full of Love and Joy. But it gives the appearance as though it has forgotten it; then to re-experience this Love and Joy, it creates sense organs, sense objects, stumbles quite a bit along the way, and finally comes to experience itself, *Appadi!* (a sound of relief): After such a long journey I have found home!

It is like a child playing on the beach. It will build a house of sand. It will enjoy building it, and it will enjoy the house. Won't let anyone come near it in case they might break it. But after it has enjoyed playing with the sand house, the child itself will destroy it. There is joy in that destruction too. That's the game. 'I won't let others even steal the joy of destroying it!'

SC: So, Atma also plays with its creations similarly.

Mahaprabu: The child I am talking about is who?? Atma. Don't think 'child' is a separate entity from Atma. IT IS ATMA. It is a sample. Like that, Atma is taking so many appearances and exhibiting its nature through those appearances. What is its purpose? In creating, protecting and destroying, in all three acts its purpose is Joy. Like that child. (Laughing!!) If Joy was in the house, will it break the house? Was there joy in the sand? No. The Atma appearing as a child, brings out Joy through sand. It uses the play with sand to bring out that in-built joy, *ananda.* Like that, Atma uses everything in the world. This is how Atma, appearing as all this, is playing every moment, with everything, using various bodies. Once it is done playing, just as the child destroyed the house and moved on, it destroys the body and moves on!!! So, IT enjoyed creating the body, enjoyed protecting the body, and enjoys destroying the body. (Laughing!)

There is no loss in it at all for Atma. It is playing for fun. We cry and say 'the body is gone' after death, but really is that true? It becomes ash and is still there. *Just like when someone destroys the house built by the child and the child cries 'Oh the house is gone', the mother says, 'Look, it didn't go anywhere. The house is in the sand only! Build another one!'*

See how it is giving examples when I talk to you!

So, we all have that love in us, just like there is air. But it needs to flow a bit to give joy as a breeze. The love in us is there. It needs to be kindled to be brought out. All this knowing, thinking, performing is for what? What is the purpose? It is to bring out the Love so that it can enjoy the Love. It is experiencing it. Enjoying it.

What is Awakening?

SC: Is awakening then the final love?

Mahaprabu: Here is what awakening is. Everything I've said so far is a result of awakening only. While saying it also there is a continuous flow of Love and it is being enjoyed! I am enjoying it continuously. Because, I am centered correctly and aligned, i.e. "knowing-thinking-performing is purely to bring out the love and enjoy the happiness" – this is in alignment in me before, during, and after I speak with you. That is awakening. You on the other hand, have heard all of this, but the alignment is missing. Still you have to awaken.

SC: Understood, but awakening also is part of the play of Atma right?

Mahaprabu: Laughing... You have asked this question earlier also. You just are asking it in a different way. See how you are thinking too much. If I tell you 'Yes, awakening also is part of the play of Atma,' you will say 'Then why bother? It will happen one day.' Look closely. Part-and-parcel of that awakening process is what is happening now!! We are talking as part of that process! This did not happen earlier. It is happening now! So to answer your question, Yes, Awakening which is part of the play of Atma is happening now! But if you start thinking, 'Let it awaken.' you will come right back into Maya. The Guru is trying to get you out of Maya. So don't think too much! (Laughing).

Everything is moving correctly. I am sharing what happened in my experience. You have listened to everything. Is there anything you have not understood? No. Clearly, you have understood. Then what is the difference between you and me? It is this: Several moments are ahead. Today, tomorrow, etc. Each and every one of those moments is the exact same for me. The next second, day, week, and year are all the same for me as it is NOW. But will it be like that for you?

SC: No. I see. For me the understanding is knowledge, and not a steady experience.

Mahaprabu: What I told you is a wonderful Truth. Nothing more needs to be said to make you understand. Beyond that, I cannot tell you the experience of Awakening. All I can say is that, if you Awaken, you will feel like I feel. If not, you will feel like you feel right now. From this we can tell, awakening has not happened in you. But it will happen. The only faith is: "We are with an Awakened One."

Why Faith is needed

Here is the problem: *Let's say a blind person is with someone who can see. How should the blind man feel?* Happy. Because he is with someone with eyes! But what does he think about the other person? How do I know that he can see? (Laughing!!) Only if I know he can see, I will believe him!!

(SC: Beautiful example. There is no way you can prove it to him that you can see. Since he is blind! Mahaprabu was laughing so much.) Yes! Write this example down and stick it somewhere! The title can be 'Why faith is needed.' *A blind man says to his friend: You are telling me you can see and that you can save me. But how do I know you can see? (Laughing!!).*

For example, let's say the man who can see takes the blind man somewhere. On the way say there are holes and dents in the ground. The friend who can see, will guide the blind man carefully through them. But as soon as the blind one feels the ground going in, he shouts 'Hey, can't you see? It appears to be a hole.' So, the blind one doubts the one who can see! Now, if the one who can see is intelligent, he will never prove to the blind that he can see. Why? Because he can never prove it. Only if he is a fool would he try to prove it. But the blind one will continuously use all situations to prove to himself that the other person is blind too! This is the situation between disciple and Guru!!! At every step the Guru will never try to prove that he is awakened. And at every step the disciple will doubt him. So what does the Guru do? He works to develop faith in the disciple. Till then it is difficult.

When will the faith develop? As long as there is doubt, you are not even in the zone of faith. How can there be doubt and faith at the same time? So, first he has to come out of all doubt. The absence of doubt is faith! It is like this. *As the blind one struggles, watching his struggles the one who can see sheds tears of compassion. Then the blind one touches the face of the companion and feels the tears. That is when he realizes, 'Oh God, how much compassion he has for me. How much he has worked for me.' Then alone, faith starts.* Similarly, only when the disciple comes to realize how much the Guru is working hard (*padaadha paadu padarar*) for the disciple's sake, only then faith and love will develop in him. But initially how it is? The disciple feels the Guru is making the disciple's life really hard!! (*padaadha paadu paduthhurar*).

Once the disciple's knowing-thinking-performance process learns that 'He is not making my life really hard; He is working really hard for me. It is Me who has made His life really hard', (Laughing!) that is the breaking point; the melting point. That is the point where he breaks. Now you tell me, can this be forced to happen? Can it happen by understanding? No. It takes its own time. You cannot force it. I cannot prove it. So, that is where Grace comes into play.

See how much patience the Guru must have. Tremendous patience. He knows the disciple doesn't have faith. He cannot prove it to him. He will be patient, knowing that once the disciple knows, he will change totally; he will know how helpful the Guru has been, and how distrustful he himself has been; Then he will truly realize that he has been blind! He will feel the real blindness. Until then he wouldn't have felt so bad about his blindness. But now he realizes: Not only have I been blind physically. I have been blind mentally too.

So, just being quietly in surrender is the only work. Otherwise, the entire life will go in distrust of the Master. Finally, when he realizes that 'Oh! So much time I wasted. Now I can see.' That is the moment of Awakening. That is Enlightenment. This is what the Guru tries to do through this relationship.

Nallapadiya nadakkatum. (May all happen well), Love you so much. Gurudeva. With these words Sri Mahaprabu ended the call.

August 13th, 2021
Phone call from Sri Mahaprabu while he was driving.

Maya, Mind and World

A very important understanding about Maya is revealed by Sri Mahaprabu. Yet another in-depth discussion when he called me from his workplace! Without missing a single task on his end, despite so many interruptions he devoted over an hour to move his disciple further towards the goal. With this understanding one is better equipped to come out of Maya.

There is only the *Uyir* (Life Energy). When I say Mind, from my point of view, I mean this: When the *Uyir*, this life energy starts flowing, then you can call it Mind. It is just a name we give to this state. When the mind stops flowing it is called *Uyir*. So, *Uyir* is another name for mind and mind is another name for *Uyir*. It is the same thing but in different states. *It is like when the water flows from the mountain it is called a river. At the edge of the mountain, it is called a waterfall. But both are same! Though both are the same, there is a difference in their utility. Just as we are able to find differences in the river vs. waterfalls.* (Sri Mahaprabu immediately quoted from the Ribhu Gita to support this definition)

Essential verses from the Ribhu Gita

There is a verse in the Ribhu Gita: (#16.19)

Anaga arivana para brahmam thane, aviddhaiyinal asaivurumel manadhai thotrum

Vinavum arivana para brahman thane, viddhayinal asaivarumel parameyagum

When you are careless (i.e. without *V zipppu Unarvu*, Awareness) IT appears as mind, IT is called as mind. This is the definition of mind. THAT itself appears as mind when you are not in *Vizippu unarvu*. But if you were conscious, aware, without oscillation, THAT reveals as Brahmam.

When Brahmam oscillates, it is Mind. When it stops it is Brahmam. Now you can relate it to the water example above. Such a big Ribhu Gita. Mahaprabu has chosen this one song out of so many verses and has given it the name "*Brahma Sutram*", the formula to attain Brahman.

And that verse continues:

Manadhadhuvum salanamudan irrukkum agil magathana jiva, para jagamai thotrum

Mind (defined as that when Brahmam flows, i.e. when you don't have *Vizippu unarvu*) when it oscillates, it appears as *Jiva* (individual) and *Jagat* (world).

Manadhaduve salanamilla irukkum agil, masatra arivana parameyamal.

When it is not oscillating, it stands as untainted wisdom, that is the Supreme Power.

It was in 2011 while I was chanting during Satsang that a single verse (mentioned at the beginning of this talk) stood out to me as the essence of the Ribhu Gita, as the formula for success. Right then I named it *Brahma Sutram*.

And this verse is important too: (#35.24)

Sathiyamai Jagathumudhal irukkum agil salanmara suzhupthiyilum irukkavendum

If there was really a world, if it really had life energy, if it had a connection with you, if you were it, then you should feel the world in deep sleep.

Ithanaiyum suzhupthiyinil ilamayale, ivai yavum kanavenave midhai endrum

Since they are not there in deep sleep, these are all *mithya*, dream, or unreal.

The next one is even better: (#35.25)

Manadhinudaya viruthi udippadarku munnum, matrandha viruthhi nasithitta pinnum

Thinai alavum illadha saga jivadhi...

Before the arising of a thought in you, and after the ending of a thought in you, there is not even a bit of individual, world, etc. *Thinai* means smaller than a mustard seed. Not even that much of *Jiva* and *Jagat* is there. When there are no thoughts in you, in that space before a thought arises or in that space between two thoughts are you able to feel the world? There is not even a trace of the world.

thiyangu mano viruttiyinaal madhiyathil

ganamadhuvai iruppadhu pol thotri nalum kalangamura sodhikkil illai yendre

In that middle state, when thoughts are there, you feel heavily (*ganam*) that you and the world exist. Everything appears in that state alone. So *Jagam* (world) and *Jivam* (individual) are where? They are only as 'thoughts' in you. Sincerely, honestly investigate this and you will find that they are not there. If those thoughts were not there, in what state would you be? A state where there is neither *Jagat* nor *Jiva*. But something IS there. You can feel it. It is in that state alone that everything exists! But you are thinking the opposite. That the World and *Jiva* are real. But they aren't. They are mere products of your fiction.

Maya and the correction

Call the thoughtless state as X.

Call Jagat thoughts as Y and

Call Jiva thoughts as Z.

What Ribhu Gita is saying is this. When you are in the thoughtless state X, there is neither Y nor Z. Then what was there? This X that is in you is what is actually there everywhere. X alone is there everywhere. That which you think and refer to as Y and Z is really all X. So, through your thoughts, you are referring to all other X as Y and Z. (SC: Amazed at the use of his words 'all other X' because we may think of Y and Z as other than X but really they are nothing but X, so he says 'all other X' even though it doesn't make sense from a language perspective) Actually Y and Z are not.

SC: So even Matter i.e. all the things that we touch and feel materially is X.

Mahaprabu: Yes! It is X touching X. But you call it Sex! (Laughing)

See, Ribhu Gita says 'honestly if you investigate' because he doubts your honesty! So Y and Z are merely thoughts. Really they are not there. What is real? X is real. This is Maya. So, see where the correction should be made. In the place where there are no thoughts!

So where is Maya? It is inside everyone as thought. It is not somewhere out there. It is in us. If you realize this correctly, most of the job is done. Then you can be very careful and do something about it. But people teach the wrong thing. Woman is Maya, World is Maya, etc. If it is outside then what can you do about it? Not much.

As long as you are in Bhakti, you leave all responsibilities in the hands of God. Why do you have Bhakti in the first place? To have a darshan of God. When Bhakti matures, where will you start to see God? In yourself. First you keep God as external and you perform Bhakti. With maturity you will see God inside you. Kind of a superimposition of you and God. As you mature even more, both become the same. Only one is left. What is that? God. So in a mature, higher state, X (Godliness) alone remains. In the other two, X and Y (human nature) remain. So when Y leaves, X alone reveals. Y has become X. In Bhakti you (Y) throw the responsibility on God (X). But when Bhakti matures and there is no Y, only X is there, then the whole responsibility is on X, since we have become X. Once we know that Maya is inside us, who has control over it? Us, the Godliness. So as a God, you have to be very alert about Maya! Because at this point everything is God. So the responsibility is also on God (which is us). If someone tells you in the beginning that you are God, the responsibility is on you, it won't work. That's why Bhakti is important, to build strength and make you responsible. *It is like telling a criminal who is really dejected, that he is responsible for all his suffering. First you have to build strength in him, let him mature, and then talk about responsibility.* Like that, I'm telling you now that Maya is nowhere but inside you.

What is Maya? *Illadhada irruppadaga nenaikiradhu dhan mayai.* Thinking and taking for real that which does not exist is Maya. Y (Jagat thoughts) and Z (You: Jiva thoughts) are not there actually. Only X (the thoughtless state) is. X alone is there everywhere. But you are referring to the same X as Y and Z. It is you who is doing it. (Laughing).

SC: I, (X) have superimposed the idea of Y and Z on X. Correct?

Mahaprabu: Yes. You are doing that. Remember, you the X are defining that same X as Y and Z. This is the place where Maya comes into play. Since you alone are doing this, the correction can only happen in you. Only if you correct this, you will attain *Jnana*, *Mukti* (liberation), and realize X. Someone is needed to tell you that it is all in your hands alone. That is the Guru. Bhagavan said, 'God or Guru can only show you the way to Mukti but will not make you enlightened.' Why? Since the Maya is inside you. A Guru is needed to tell you this. When Bhagavan said 'will not' it means he cannot. It is not like he has the ability and is holding on to it.

What can be done

The great thing is that you can never lose X. It is always there. You can only lose Y and Z. And staying as X, all the activities can be done. See how much confidence this can give you. X exists throughout, whether Y and Z are not. So every moment is an opportunity to lose Y and Z, and stay in X. So have tremendous confidence. So be happy, know that X is alone is, and that Y and Z are the work of Maya. If you truly realize this, you can use Maya but Maya cannot use you. You will know when to use it and when to lose it. Step by step, step by step you will know. You will know the cause and effect of Maya, the necessity of Maya. Mahaprabu also was in the trap of it. Now that he is free from it, he knows that it is all the play of Maya, yet he is neither against Maya nor stuck in it. In other words, once you are freed from it you will never again be trapped in it. It is like this: *Without knowing that you are a rich man you have been living as a beggar. But so much evidence has been given to you that you really are a king. And once you have realized it, they have placed you on the throne. Now you live like a king, but you still know what begging is. You will not beg, but you are not against it. Even if you are forced to beg, you will never believe that you are a beggar. You will always know that you are the king. But before knowing you are a king, you were totally identified with a beggar. Similarly once you are freed from Maya, you will not go back.*

SC: Since Y and Z are not actually there, is it better to not put the effort toward losing Y and Z and instead put effort into retaining X?

Mahaprabu: Both should happen side by side. Sometimes, when you are in Y and Z and stuck in Maya, then you should bring to remembrance that Y and Z are not real. That is all you can do at that point since you have lost touch with X. If you are able to be in X at all times, which is Unarvin Thodarbu – my *tharaka mantra*! then it is great. But when your wife and children appear, will you retain X? No. So at those points bring to consciousness that Y and Z are not there. That which doesn't exist is not there. Instead of saying only That exists (X) you can say, that which does not exist is not there!! In other words, instead of saying only X is there, you are saying Y and Z are not there.

SC: It sounds very clear in theory, but practically it is difficult.

Mahaprabu: Practically also it is very easy, but it is a matter of interest. That's why Buddha said, "I said everyone can attain Jnana, it is possible. But whether all are interested? That is the question". See how deeply he has found this.

SC: So that is where the Guru comes in, to kindle that interest!

Mahaprabu: What do you think I am doing now!!! (Laughing) I am in the college right now. So many works are happening. People come to me for guidance. I give them. Phone calls come. I attend. All this is going on. But the main work is happening! The main course! (Referring to him talking to me)

SC: (thinking to himself) What a detailed, in-depth explanation about Brahman, Maya, World, etc. that Sri Mahaprabu is giving, all while working in the college as the head of the department! I could hear so many interruptions and phone calls that he attends to without any frustration whatsoever, and yet he ALWAYS picks up exactly where he left our conversation, never missing even once. When the facade of individuality has disappeared, this must be how the Supreme Power operates in a body. In total perfection.

Mahaprabu: Always see yourself as a skeleton. When the wife appears, when the children appear, see them all as skeletons. That will help. It is like this: *You have painted a house in beautiful colours. It gets etched in your memory that you are living in such a beautiful home. If you paint all the rooms white you will be less attracted. If you didn't paint them at all and just left all the bricks exposed along with the concrete floor, would you consider it a palace? It is the same home. But if you see it as bricks, will you be enamored by it?*

So try seeing yourself and everyone as skeletons. Try it. Only you can do all this!! Not anyone else. I can give you all the answers but you have to write the exam in your handwriting! In your name. Your share has to be done.

Write this down clearly somewhere:

I should always remember the answer to these 2 questions:

Where is Maya? (In me)

Who is responsible? (I am).

September 17th, 2021
Phone call from Sri Mahaprabu while he was at his work place..

Note: Sri Mahaprabu spoke about the importance of chanting Ribhu Gita and reminisced about the days when he would go for Ribhu Gita chanting at 5 AM every day. For this, he would have to wake up at 3:45 AM, take bath, get ready, purchase flowers and travel to the place it was being chanted to be there by 5 AM. And how many were there? Just two. The person conducting it in his house and Mahaprabu. In a tiny room, roughly 6 ft by 5 ft. For one hour the chanting would go on. This continued for nearly 2 years without break, from 1997-98. Bhagavan used to say, chanting the Ribhu Gita can be equivalent to Samadhi. After enlightenment I find that there are verses in the Ribhu Gita that bring me to tears. Once in 2008, I sang an entire chapter and from the first verse itself, tears started to flow like a waterfall, till the last verse.

Awareness and Compassion

We have become habitual to doing things without attentiveness, and worse we are not aware of the Awareness which is what makes everything possible. And that Awareness is full of Love. Sri Mahaprabu stresses the importance of being aware, moment to moment.

Mahaprabu asked a disciple: Your hands are moving. Did you observe them?

This is what we are asking people here to practice. These are parts of 'your' body. For example, Your neck is slanted right now. Are you aware of it? You are talking to me, but you are not aware of the slanted neck. If you were aware of it, what would you do? You would straighten it. Because, is it healthy to sit for long with a slanted neck? No. If I spoke to you for a long time with my neck slanted, how would you feel? So what is needed is Gavanam, Awareness. So, if only we bring Gavanam, Awareness into our lives, wherever things are crooked (aren't right), they will all be 'straightened' out!

Being Aware of Awareness

Therefore, staying in Awareness is called Dhyanam. But what do people think? Sitting in a room for an hour is Dhyanam. That is not Dhyanam. Is sitting in a room for an hour enough? No. When is Awareness needed? In every action, in every second. Whoever is attentive every second, in every action, only those are in Dhyanam.

We should go a bit deeper. Can the hand be aware? No. No body part can be aware or attentive. Yet there is Awareness. Is there a relationship between Awareness and the Body? No. Awareness is different, Body is different. You can use Awareness to correct the body's state, but they are different. For example, you just scratched an itch. Why? Because the itch was brought to attention. Call the scratching action X. Who did the action? The body. Call it Y. Did the body do it by itself or did the itch come to Awareness and then the body scratched it? It was Awareness that brought the itch to attention. Call that Awareness Z. These 3 things are there in all actions. Even while you type on the computer at work. There is the act of typing, there is the computer and hands and there is also Attention, which allows you to focus on the task and do it properly. **But that Attention is not Awareness. It is not**

Meditation. Just as the attention is on typing properly, can't you have an Awareness of the hands typing, the eyes seeing? Isn't that possible? And then, can't you be Aware of that Awareness also? Yes. If you can do that, then you are in Dhyanam, Meditation.

(Clapping in the room).

While clapping, were you aware of your hands clapping? Were you aware how much sound it made? When you were clapping (X), if your attention was on the hands (Y), were you the Awareness (Z) that was aware of that attention? You see, the whole act of clapping is possible only because of what? Awareness (Z). So shouldn't we be Aware of Awareness (Z)? If you are, then it is Dhyanam. So in all actions, at all times we should not lose our Awareness of Awareness.

What causes suffering?

Once a task X is done, the body Y has no work. At that point will Awareness Z disappear? No. When there is a task, this Z dispatches the body Y to do that task X. But when X is done, Z continues to remain. But are you aware of that Awareness Z? No. **This is what causes the most suffering for us**. That is why we fear, we worry and do everything to fix that. We have missed what is there. Even for you to know you exist, what do you need? That Awareness Z. It is there but you have continuously missed it. See how important it is. It tells you that you exist. It tells you your parents exist. So, more important than your parents, more important than you, is what? That Awareness. Do you give it that importance? No. You are not even turning towards it. That needs to change. Awareness is your biggest treasure. Even though it is available 24x7 you are not experiencing it, you are not using it. Isn't that the biggest loss? That's why people suffer. We need to start using our biggest treasure more and more. As you start to use it, you will come out of suffering.

Your parents will die one day. What is that which even tells you they died? Awareness. If so, then that same Awareness will tell you when your body dies. Correct? Even the birth of your body happened in Awareness. But you were not aware of that Awareness. Imagine if you saw your body dying, in full Awareness. How much understanding you would have! Because there is no Awareness, people are terrified of death. Awareness is like a mirror. It has to be used to see the reflection. If you don't use it, it will still be there.

Just like when you walk on a road full of potholes without being attentive, you would fall into each hole and get hurt. Similarly, you have been travelling for long without Awareness and falling into potholes. **One such hole is this birth!** *You have a torchlight in your hand all the time (Awareness). Yet you are walking on a road full of potholes without using the torch, even though you keep falling and suffering. What would someone call such a person? A complete fool. So, who are we? Total fools. Even now we have that torch. So, we should start using it. The only reason we keep falling into the ditches is because we don't use the torch (Awareness).*

It takes tremendous effort. *We have gone deep into a dark and scary forest without using the torch. Then what is the way to come out? To turn on the torch and return. You are not going to come back all the way immediately. It will take time, but turning the torch on and coming out is the only way to prevent further getting lost and suffering. The torch is there always, anytime for you. You can use it any time.* The one who points this out is the Guru. Using the light of his torch, he is showing you that you have a torch too, so that you can also get back on track with your torch.

Awareness is full of Love

The eyes might stop working. Ears might stop hearing. Will Awareness stop working? No. That torch is independent. Aren't deaf or blind people still Aware? This Awareness is what Vallalar calls *Arul Perum Jyothi*, The Divine Light of Grace.

This Awareness is not just Awareness. It is full of Love. For example: *You love your son. Does that love come from the body?* No. It comes from something other than the body. Does Awareness come from the body? No. It comes from something other than the body. So isn't it likely that from the same point, the same source, both Awareness and Love arise? Yes. They are like twins. Wherever there is Awareness there is Love. Wherever there is Love, there is Awareness.

And Love has different levels. *Like water appears as drizzle, shower, heavy rain, waterfall, river, pond, ocean. All are water.* Just the name is different according to the form. Similarly Love has different strengths. When you give someone water there is some love. When someone is fainting and you help him, there is a larger degree. When Love is maximum, we call it Karunai, Total Compassion. So, where there is Awareness, there is total Compassion.

Can total compassion, the highest, purest form of Love, come from a stone idol representing God? No. But it can come from only one place. Your heart. Yet have you touched it? No. Just touching a lower degree of it, how do you feel? Happy. How about a bit stronger, when you love someone? How do you feel? More happy right? Imagine how you would feel when you experience the highest form of Love called Karunai (total compassion)! You will feel ecstatic. Where is this Karunai? Inside you!! **So, to be extremely happy you need to be totally compassionate.** And it is within you 24x7 yet you are not using it.

Start with Awareness

The effort to reach this treasure is called Dhyanam. Either you can start with Awareness or with Compassion. But we are not used to, or exposed to that level of compassion. Are our parents that compassionate to each other? To their children? No. But humans have been given all these relations so that they can enjoy the built-in compassion and live happily. Animals aren't given that. They don't have cousins and uncles and aunts! But no human is purely loving towards others. It is hard to start with Love. Plus, your mind might cheat you. For example, if I don't reciprocate your love, you will stop loving me. So especially in this Kali Yuga (the present age of the world which is in darkness), it is hard to start with Love. So it is better to start with Awareness.

Because Awareness is not related to others. It is only related to you. Within you. As you become Aware, without your knowledge your Love will increase in degrees, your happiness will increase correspondingly. You will Love without fear. Awareness brings a lack of fear. And **when you reach the peak of Awareness you will reach the peak of Compassion.**

Lord Buddha's example

The pinnacle of Awareness, Lord Buddha was also the pinnacle of Compassion. That is why he traveled to his town (years after enlightenment) without any fear. Imagine, he left his wife without notice; he left without even seeing his newborn son; he left his parents and all the responsibilities of the kingdom etc. Imagine a normal person returning to that town. Wouldn't he greatly fear his wife, his son, his father, all of whom he had terribly wronged? It was their fault that they had to suffer because of him. But not Buddha. Even though he knew that he had wronged them, he faced it all without any fear whatsoever. He went because he was full of compassion for them. And the bravery to handle every situation there, was possible for him because of his Awareness. Imagine, he was not going there alone. He went with his disciples! It did not matter in the least for him. His Compassion took him there. His Awareness removed all fear. In fact, the wife had instigated her son to question his dad strongly. Why did you leave us? But in the end, what did the wife do? She advised her son to leave her and go join his father Buddha as a disciple. He is a good man, she told him! **That is the victory for Buddha's compassion.**

Today, people don't want to be loving and compassionate. And they don't know or even care about Awareness. Yet what is it that everyone wants? To be happy all the time. How is it possible? What needs to be done is what we are doing here in Satsang. San Margam. The path of Truth.

May 8th, 2022
Rest House at Paliapattu

How Witnessing Works

A powerful talk by Sri Mahaprabu about how he sees things, how the inner system works (in the context of Brain, Awareness, Witnessing and Samadhi), and what needs to be done. A must-read!

How does a Jnani see his/her body?

Before I had not realized the Truth, I was an individual, with a mind, a thinking process, without any experience. But now in 2003 (referring to Jan 1, 2003 when Sri Mahaprabu was enlightened), I am not a person at all. There is no relation to the body at all. But I AM there. I know what I AM as. And that can never be disturbed. The body can be disturbed. You can shake it. But that which I AM, cannot be disturbed.

SC: So, do you have a feeling that YOU are contained in the body?

Mahaprabu: No, there is no relation at all between THAT and the body. It is very hard to explain. Very hard. It is somewhat like this: *There are a few empty balloons in front of you with the mouths open. Imagine that air enters them, they will float, right? Now imagine if Air had a feeling. So, Air will simply know it is there; outside the balloon and inside the balloon, equally. Then, will Air have a feeling that it is confined to the balloon? No. But if the balloon had a feeling, then the balloon would feel that something entered it. That is how the body will feel.*

So, to answer your question, THAT (referring to the Self) will not have a feeling of inside or outside the body. The Body will feel something entered into us. Is that feeling for the balloon or for THAT? The Balloon.

SC: Is that feeling for the body a permanent thing?

Mahaprabu: No. It will come, it will go. But who would be concerned with that? Air or Balloon? The balloon alone will be concerned with that. Because Air is not related to the balloon at all. In the example, *I am Air.* I have no worries about the balloon. Any bodily sensation is not mine!

SC: But the body by itself cannot sense that Air is in it right?

Mahaprabu: The brain is in the body, right? The brain will sense that Air has entered.

Awareness and the Brain

In fact, who is the one that is going to know that I am Atma, or I am Brahman? The Brain! The Brain is the one that does not know it. See, the *Param Porul* (Supreme Power), the Atma, Brahman, Self does not have a need to know that it is the Supreme Power, Atma, Self. That need would arise only if it had turned into two, the Self and Not-Self, and later it needed to know that both were the same. That is to say that for the Self to realize itself, it should have been divided into the Self and another. But is the Self divided? No. So, who needs that understanding? The brain. So, when the brain senses the air (referring to IT) entering, the brain will know. It will know when it leaves. There is no condition that it should be there always.

For example, *I have a light and something that covers it. When I cover the light, you'll see light for a specific diameter. I use a bigger cover. The lighted area will be larger. An even bigger cover will show more light.* That is how the brain will know when THAT enters. Whenever needed, a certain amount of light (Awareness) is felt by the brain. Enough amount of it to know what it needs at that moment. If more is needed, more is made available to the brain. All these are simply examples to try to make you understand.

Once the brain recognizes that there is this thing, Consciousness, Atma, Self, it will never forget IT. IT was always there but not within the recognition of the brain, which was focused entirely on the idea of a person all this while.

SC: When you say IT, you are referring to the Self, correct? Why don't you say 'I'?

Mahaprabu: Yes. See, I can use 'Me' or 'I' only when there is another! There isn't. So, it feels dirty to say 'I' or 'Me' in that sense. It is like this. Your brain has 2 hemispheres. Can the left hemisphere tell the right hemisphere: 'I' am going to eat. What are 'you' going to do? It can't even be imagined. It won't happen that way. Similarly, there is no feeling of I or me, since there isn't another. Even for you. Forget about Jnanam (enlightenment) and check. Is there one I for you or two I's? No. There is only one I at any time. You are singular, even as an ego. You say, 'I', for 'Me' etc. You don't say for 'Them'. You cannot separate it. Do you say, 'I' am hungry, but 'He' is not, while referring to yourself? (Laughing)

All this is very hard to explain and understand. Only a close example can be given. But when IT happens, the brain will understand that all the while IT was there, but not noticed. Like an amla fruit in one's palm that was always there. Once you know it is there, even if you close your fist, you will not forget that the fruit is with you now

Witness and Samadhi

SC: So there is an effort needed for the brain to recognize the Self. What is that?

Mahaprabu: At this point you need to put in effort. You have not seen yourself. You have been told that there is something. You feel your existence, you can find it, but you don't know much about it. You haven't brought it within the total awareness of the brain. So, as you keep familiarizing your brain towards it more and more, certain experiences will happen. Initially when experiences happen to you, something is witnessing the experience. Who is that witness? The Brain. But when the Brain turns off, there is no witness at all. That is SAMADHI. So, Samadhi is a happening. After coming out of Samadhi, there is someone, a witness to recollect and say that I only knew what was happening up to a point. After a point I don't know what happened. Who is that witness? The Brain. That witness is a very subtle ego. It was the ego that was searching to go deep. It is a minor portion of the ego. At some point the brain will learn that 'I' is just a thought, a record.

As you go more often into Samadhi, there will still be two things. The tiny ego as the last witness, and a happening that takes place after that (Samadhi). So, will you prefer the witnesser or the experience that follows it? The Experience. But now you are still enjoying being the witness. Yes or No?

SC: Yes, I find myself hanging around as the witness when trying to go deeper. Waiting for the experience to happen, to enjoy it!

Mahaprabu: Yes, so how can there be an experience as long as you are there! But there is no other way. This is how it happens. Again and again, you try to witness yourself going into Samadhi, and when Samadhi happens you lose yourself. Can the witness tell what happens in Samadhi? No. The witness turns off. Only in Samadhi is IT there totally. It goes to the Origin, Adi. Since it is equal to the origin, it is called Samadhi (Sama means equal and Adi means origin). *Adhikku samam* – Equal to the Origin. So IT is the Origin. Hence the word Samadhi. IT will be in the universal state, where the witness no longer exists, and you as an individual will disappear. So, in that starte will you have any relation to this body? Will you care to enter it? And does it matter whether the body is there or not? Death doesn't bother you anymore. Similarly, birth doesn't matter to you either. All this will become registered by who? That last witness. It will fully absorb the fact that birth and death are all for the body alone. Not for THAT state. The witness will no longer care about body, birth or death.

SC: So then, the Realization is for the Witness, a part of the brain system.

Mahaprabu: Yes, who does the thinking? The brain.

SC: Yes, in the brain is recorded a thought that I am the witness.

Mahaprabu: Yes, these thoughts of individual, and now the thought of a witness are all where? In the brain. They are all recorded in the brain. That's why in the olden days they didn't encourage looking in the mirror at all. But see today. Continuously we are recording images of the body as ourself!

SC: So last time we met I remember sitting in the car (after the *Unarvu nilai dhyanam* – practice of feeling ones Existence, you gave me) and not knowing anything for the next 30 minutes. There was a peace throughout. The car reached home and that's when I became aware. Does that mean I was in Samadhi?

Mahaprabu: Yes, you were but you didn't realize it. That is why you are doubting it. If the witness was really sharp, it would know what happened at that point of disappearance, and the point of reappearance. As you do it more and more, the witness becomes sharper, becomes more familiar with it, becomes really sharp. Then it will know the point where you disappeared into Samadhi and the point where you came out of it. If it did, you wouldn't doubt if you were in Samadhi. But that is how it happens. Over repeated practice, the witness becomes sharp.

SC: Also, the witness is not familiarized fully with that Experience; it doesn't know that it is always there like fruit in the palm.

Mahaprabu: Yes. As Bhagavan said (Mahaprabu narrated a verse in Tamil, about being a sharp witness, which I later found to be verse 28 in *Ulladu Narpadu* which you can find here: https://shlokam.org/ulladu-narpadu-explained). The meaning is this:

Controlling speech and breath, and diving deep within oneself — like one who, to find a thing that has fallen into water, dives deep down – one must seek out the source whence the aspiring ego springs.

Bhagavan is referring to that sharp witness. (Mahaprabu kept stressing the word sharp witness, to me again and again.)

As you go more and more into *Samadhi*, the witness will become very familiar with the Experience. That will take you there more and more. As soon as it senses IT, it will make arrangements to dive deep. Like *when the Chief Minister comes, people clear the path quickly for him to pass through!* You will not interact much with the world.

So tell me, who enjoys the Experience?

SC: The Witness.

All this while who had suffered?

SC: The same Witness.

Yes, the one who saw *Naragam* (hell), now sees *Swargam* (Heaven). Only he would know comparatively that this is Heaven.

This is why you cannot help those who are suffering in the world. They have to go to the extreme of suffering to turn the other direction. So many of you run to help someone who is suffering. Is that a good thing? You are stopping what nature is doing. We don't let people suffer. The witness there needs to know the extreme of suffering to turn towards Happiness. As far as Brahmam is concerned, there is no Heaven or Hell. All this is just for the Witness.

Once the Witness has seen the real Swargam (figuratively heaven, but means the Truth, the Experience), will he see the Naragam (figuratively hell) in the world as Naragam?

He will never see this as hell again, because he knows that this suffering is not real. When I see someone suffering, I see it as part of the Play, for him to turn inward. Once you have seen THAT which is appearing as all this, will you then feel bad? This Naragam (hell) is a play, and it is created so the individual can turn inward. I see this as compassion. I am seeing it from the standpoint of the Air (balloon example above). It is everywhere, just appearing different.

Keep the Witness sharp

The Witnessing needs to be very sharp. That's why you should not see things unnecessarily, talk to people unnecessarily. Do you have one Witness or many! So, with the only Witness you have, when you engage it in so many things, seeing things and talking about things, imagine the quality of that Witnessing. It would be very dull. As you feed more and more information, at some point you will say 'What Witness, What are you talking about? I don't feel any Witness'. Imagine the plight of one who does not even know there is a witness!

Imagine the plight of students today. So much information is fed into them continuously by parents, teachers, friends etc. What potential can you expect from them? The goal seems to be to make them efficient, not Aware. Like a military man, who is efficient, and disciplined. When he becomes an officer, who do you think he is going to create? More efficient beings. Like an IAS officer (a senior officer in the government). His entire life will centre around that role, and not who he really is. And people around him are continuously feeding him information that strengthens the role. And these so-called successful people become role models for others. *It is like they are all drinking from a mirage and saying 'Ahh, my thirst is gone', so now others learn to drink from that mirage.*

Thus, the Witness becomes duller and duller as one engages in the world. By Witness I mean an ability, a witnessing ability. A dead brain (referring to just the organ) cannot witness anything. Brahman alone gives it the light, which enlivens it to receive and store information. Brahman itself empowers the Brain by giving it an ability to Witness IT (Brahman).

In this day and age, safeguarding that Witness is very difficult. Who alone can have the Experience? The Witness alone can. But in the crowded world we live in, no one is witnessing. You don't even know what is going on in your mind or your body because your attention is always turned outward. After going inward, you have to cross what is in your body, in your mind and in your emotions. It takes a very sharp witness to go past this and start to experience what reality IS.

It is the nature of the witness to run after whatever comes in its view.

SC: And if there isn't anything in view, it starts to ruminate on the past or imagine the future.

Mahaprabu: Yes. That is why the present-moment practice is very essential. Remember I told you about the practice I had in 2002 for one full year to be in the present moment. Also, this witnessing ability, in rare cases suddenly touches on the Experience. But that is like Sartori. It is not necessarily repeatable. So, the only way is to keep on sharpening the witness till the point where it not only sees the Experience but becomes stable in it.

The Importance of Patience

Even then, can the Witness create the Experience of Samadhi? No. Therefore you can only make the Witnessing ability sharp. Only up to that point is your job. After that, the Experience (samadhi) may happen or may not happen. That is why tremendous patience is needed. Witnessing ability is one thing. Keeping yourself patient is another ability. Both of these have to be developed simultaneously and that's how they develop. They are related. In this world do you think people are being taught to be patient? No. But the very first ability that needs to be developed is Patience. It is the mother of so many abilities, including Witnessing. So, the very first thing that the Master develops in a disciple is Patience. He puts the disciple through increasing levels of trials to grow his patience. Many disciples lose their patience. Their interest in Spirituality grows, but their abilities are not growing. Look within yourself keenly and tell me, do you have all the patience it requires to reach what I am referring to?

SC: No.

Mahaprabu: Then how can it Happen? Whoever you are, you may be a beggar, you may be a king. It doesn't matter. The requirement is the same. And I cannot give you a portion of my patience. It has to be developed. That is what the Guru is doing.

And you know the interesting thing, this Patience ability should be developed quickly. We cannot grow it very patiently (laughing). The body has been given limited time. If you are really patient, won't it reflect in all your actions? It is a good thing. And it has to be developed. There is no other way. Ask any human mind, which one it prefers to reward. One with patience or one who is impatient? You will pick the patient one and give him the prize. Now imagine, you are asking for the HIGHEST prize of all. Imagine how much patience you have to develop. Only when you have done that, will IT notice you and come to you oozing.

[Mahaprabu then spoke about his vision to have a school where children are taught these Godly qualities from young. And how parents are likely to be the first resistance. Therefore, he is looking at bringing orphans in.]

June 28th, 2022
Sithhalapakkam House

The 3rd One

In this talk, Sri Mahaprabu clearly shows what actually is existing but instead how we are leading our lives as though we exist as individuals, and that we control things. He gave us practical tips on how to come out of this gigantic misconception.

Only two things are here

One is the body made up of bones and flesh. The other is the Awareness or Attention which is made up of Love and Knowledge. So Attention is not a raw, dry one. It contains Love as its juice, and it has Self-Knowledge also. It is not made of flesh. The body is made of flesh and bone. The body does not have any Attentiveness, doesn't have any Love and doesn't have any Knowledge. So, only these two things are here. We should have a clear understanding about this. Only 2 things are there.

The body, it may give some trouble which we can manage, which we can accept, or it has to be accepted. A little disturbance. And is manageable. There is no disturbance from the 2nd one, the nameless, formless one, the attentiveness, filled with love and self-knowledge. No disturbance from it.

Together, these 2 things which are existing here and now really don't give you much suffering. But if you look back at your history, the quantity of your suffering, the duration of suffering in this lifetime that you have suffered, is not because of these two. Where is all this suffering coming from? The 3rd one. Which is an imaginary one. That I am an individual; I am so and so; I have to be like this; I should not be like this; I like this; I don't like this; I am a man; I am a female; I am rich; I am poor; I am not enlightened. All these things collectively are called as 'Idea that you are an individual'. This is the 3rd one. It is not real. It doesn't have any real existence. You cannot show it. You cannot feel it. You can show the body, touch and feel it. And you are able to feel the existence which is nameless and formless which has tremendous attentiveness, with love, which is called Sat Cit Anandam. So these two things are here.

These 2 things never produce this unbearable suffering. Never. Then where from is this Suffering which has affected you, coming? Where from? From imagination. The imaginary 'I'. As this 'I' is imaginary, all the suffering produced by it in my point of view is also imaginary. If you can stay without the imaginary 'I' you can stay without suffering. This is the formula. You need not read the entire Ribhu Gita or Kaivalya Navaneetam, the entire Tiruvarutpa, need not read the entire Tiruvasagam if you are able to understand and accept the simple truth that the suffering you have experienced so far is not because of these 2 things which are really existing. So the sufferings are imaginary. As we do not have the wisdom, the knowledge, as we are living with an imagination, the suffering is also imagination. This you should clearly understand.

To get that understanding first you have to accept my words with faith, and sincerity. If you are able to do that, there is no need for anything else. As you are not honestly accepting and as you are not honestly analyzing, as you are not really interested in experiencing the reality 100%, as it takes time to prepare you, to fill that time I have to sing Tiruvasagam, Tiruvarutpa, Ramana Geetham, Ribhu Gita, Avudayakkal, Naradeva and now Kaivalya. All these are coming and standing in line! When you are preparing yourself, when you come in line with the Master, when you have only this desire to know and feel this reality, then you will be in the same line as the Master. At that time all these things (reading etc.) are not needed. Just you have to understand that all suffering is imaginary.

A very big dream

You may feel the suffering. *It is like a man who is dreaming that he is pregnant and he is experiencing severe pains during the delivery.* In the dream he will feel that the delivery pains are real. But when he comes out of the dream, the pains he felt, the pains that he thought were real have no value. The same thing is happening here. You are in a dream. In that dream you are experiencing the suffering. When the man dreams that he has delivery pain, in his dream he feels his body moving, and he is trying to put his hand on his stomach and starts groaning Ah! Ah! But he is dreaming. Now it is exhibited in the outer body too. Now, say you are looking at the man. By his actions you can understand that he is dreaming that he has delivery pains. You know then that the only way to help him is to make him come out of the dream. Not by helping fix his dream-pain. Only by making him come out of the dream can you make him come out of his delivery pain, which is just part of a dream.

I am trying to pull you out of the dream. You are in a dream. A very big, continuous, strong dream. Your pain is a dream. Your pain is imaginary. Just stay with me. It is enough.

You have to understand this carefully. Many people easily dismiss the whole world as a dream, I am a dream, you are a dream. That is not true. You are born into a womb, you can touch and feel the body, you can feel your existence, the attention, the love. All these are there. The Supreme Power that created all this is experiencing its creation through the body. All this is good. What is a dream, what is imaginary is the idea that you are a person, an entity that is separate from the creator and its creation. As a result, you carry the burden every single moment of trying to survive this life. That is painful. You are going through life as though you are doing it all even though in reality IT is doing it all. You CAN go through the same life without the idea that you are an individual, without the idea that you are doing it all (since you are NOT doing it anyway). But since this idea is strongly enmeshed in our brains over many lives, we seem unable to make this separation. That is the problem. Be very clear about it. That you are an individual is the dream.

If I ask you to point out, you will show the body and you can feel the one that listens. The 3rd one is imaginary. Joanne, the doctor, the wife, the female, the mother. But you can't point out Joanne. It is just thought. It is a record. It is mere information stored in the brain. You can use it, but it is not the reality of who you are.

Like I said earlier, the body can cause some trouble due to age and therefore gives a bit of suffering over time. It can be managed. The one which is behind, the second component, the listener, never gives any trouble. It will not give you any suffering. But if you take your whole life see how much more suffering you have experienced, compared to the little happiness. To attain that little happiness, you have suffered a lot. All that suffering originates from the 3rd one. The 3rd one is a record. An imagination. It is not real. And since the suffering originates from 3rd one whose basis is not real, then the suffering that originates from it also is unreal, an imagination. You can keep on fighting to minimize the suffering, saying 'we should not suffer', 'we should not suffer' but what about the reality of the suffering? It occurs only because you have accepted the 3rd one as real. Now we have to learn how to live without the 3rd one. Unconsciously we have accepted the 3rd one. Consciously we have to deny. This is the real practice. Always try to remain as the reality. The Awareness and the body.

Surrender is the way out

No mantra and no books are going to help. Only the Master to whom you surrender totally, only the Master who is interested in lifting you up, alone can help. And surrender is always to one Master. For example, imagine a woman surrendering to her mother and her husband. She will get two different instructions for each thing. How will she live? So true surrender is to one Master and that alone will work. Your surrender creates the responsibility for the Master to help you. If he does not have the assurance from you that you are sincere in your surrender, then he cannot work with you. And seeing different Masters and sitting with them is like going on spiritual tours. It's like going to different shopping malls. One can love and have relationships with many spiritual beings, and that is different. Working for enlightenment is entirely different. Loving is different from submitting. Enlightenment needs submission. Submission can be done to one only. Not with many. If you surrender to the Master and you are single-pointed about knowing the Truth, the help from the Master will come; that surrender will take you to the Source.

Living with a Master is like taking a new birth in a different world but with the same body. That is the difficulty. You have the same brain, so everything has to be unlearned. Just by unlearning, this learning can happen.

You have to become a child, a newborn. The Master is both the Father and Mother. Don't accept the 3rd one. As much as you are reducing the 3rd one, your suffering will be reduced. It is proportionate. You cannot avoid your body on your own. You cannot avoid the one which is listening. But you can avoid the 3rd one. That alone is possible. It alone should be done. As you begin to come out of the suffering that is caused by the 3rd one you will feel tremendous energy. You won't feel tired. Now by feeling that strength in you, the shifting from the body to THAT which is the 2nd one will become very easy. It is the tiredness due to the suffering caused by the 3rd one that is not giving us the strength to shift. So the first job is to reduce the suffering. For this, we have to reduce the connection with the 3rd one. This is in your hands. Since it is in your hands alone, no Master is able to do this for you. Because the interest to accept or reject the 3rd one is with you. The Master cannot enter into this freedom and he should not. If he does enter, it will affect your psychology. That is why a real Master will not enter. It is you who have to strongly decide to reduce the link with the 3rd one. Only then will your suffering be reduced. In this way, you can develop the strength. What you need is strength. Without understanding this deeply, people are trying to develop strength in so many ways like going to ashrams, visiting natural places, doing charitable deeds, etc. But instead of developing the strength, unknowingly they are becoming weak because by doing all these things they are keeping in touch with whom? The 3rd one! 'I am going to this ashram, I have donated this and that, I have met that Master.' As your link to the 3rd one increases, your suffering increases. You are reducing your chance to shift. After a point you cannot return. You become like plastic. Your elasticity has gone. You cannot do anything after that. You have to throw it out. Nature will press the refresh button. A restart. A new birth.

Silence. Don't chase it.

You can sit for a long time in meditation, you can sit in Satsang like this by showing an interest to be silent. And just because you feel silence it doesn't mean you have disconnected from the 3rd one. Feeling silence and disconnecting from the 3rd one is entirely different. By disconnecting from the 3rd one, as your imaginary suffering gets reduced, as you are more in the real system, due to that you will become silent. Attaining silence in that manner is what is real. It is the effect. Not the aim. Your aim should be to disconnect the 3rd one, and not to feel the silence. As you have disconnected you will feel the silence. But seekers generally give importance to silence. They chase silence. Disconnection is the key. Not silence. Because it is Disconnection that brings the real Silence. Many are deceiving themselves by chasing silence. 'I went there and it was so peaceful. I felt so silent.' What is the use? After coming out of that place or out of that Satsang you will immediately engage with the 3rd one. And as you are again engaging with the 3rd one, once again you are engaging with suffering. Then your mind will find a new place. A new silence. But that too is temporary. The mind says, 'Let us go to another place'. And so on. One day the body will die. Please understand. Who wants that silence? The 3rd one! Before going for wisdom, please understand your foolishness.

See, as you are here in Satsang you don't need to think you are a doctor, a female, a wife, etc. Without these thoughts you can stay here. Staying here and now without the 3rd one is the practice. Not attaining silence. You need not seek silence. You need not beg for silence. Silence will seek you. It will come and reach you. All you have to do is disconnect with the 3rd one continuously. And if and when you experience silence, enjoy it but don't go behind it. Don't try for it. Next time you catch yourself engaging with the 3rd one, simply remember again to disconnect from it. Come out immediately. Again, the silence will prevail. Enjoy it. But don't try for it. Your only attempt in life is to disengage with the 3rd one. So far in life, you have been making attempts to engage with so many things, so many people and events. This is your last attempt. And it is to not engage with the 3rd one. By repeatedly making the attempt not to engage, you will become disengaged.

Reduce contacts

And we have to reduce contact as much as possible, especially with human beings. Limit contacts to the very minimum required for the survival of the body and for continuing the spiritual journey. All other contacts are hindrances and obstacles. Because they continuously remind you of the 3rd one. Reduce the contact to just that which is needed for the survival of the body. All extra contacts are a hindrance. Ignorance is a highly contagious disease, highly infectious. So, keep yourself away from worldly contacts as much as possible. Depending on your need you should have the minimum. No extra. And maximize the attention here on Satsang with the Master. That is the perfect balance. Not 50%–50%. Maximum here, minimum there.

You yourself cannot forget the 3rd one. *It is like a baby who is used to feeding from the mother. After a point when it is time for the baby to move away from that source and give it solid food, the baby will still insist on the mother's milk. Due to habit. It will not even consider anything else. The mother has to take measures, sometimes extreme measures to wean the baby away from breast feeding, such as applying neem paste to that area so the baby will feel disgusted while trying to suck!* That is the only way. How will the baby on its own forget the strong habit and move away from it? It won't happen. Similarly, the Master will take the steps necessary for you to drop the old habit, disconnecting from that 3rd one.

Every Satsang is a festival. These are celebratory moments. Just by seeing the Master, we can recollect our real nature. And by being with the Master it becomes stronger.

Love You. Love You All.

◆ ◀◀ ◆ ▶▶ ◆

July 15th, 2022
Rest House at Paliapattu

ABCD's

Using the four letters A, B, C, D to denote the various components of our natural system i.e. Atma, Body, Vasanas and Ego, Sri Mahaprabu gives a clear-cut understanding of the problem we are stuck in, and the solution to come out of it. A must-read for all seekers.

During Satsang, a disciple (D) who has known Mahaprabu for some time said: 'I am in a tough situation. I am in love with someone. I don't know what to do. I am wondering who is that love for. Who is having that Love?

Mahaprabu responded by saying 'Love can be there. You can also love her, but you should not think of her as your lover (*kaadhali*).' How this is possible, is how the discussion started.

D: How is that possible Mahaprabu? Say in my house there is a toilet. If I think it is mine, I will maintain it well. But if it is a public toilet, I won't maintain it well. So only if I think of it as mine, I will maintain it well. You are asking me to maintain it without thinking of it as mine.

Mahaprabu: Don't think of Public vs. Private toilets. *Say they have given a public toilet in the street and in each house also there have allocated a toilet but you don't own it. There are 100 homes in the street and each house has been allocated a toilet. The toilet is in your house, but you don't own it. It is not in your name. Now is that a public or private toilet?*

D: Public.

Mahaprabu: (Laughing) So can you own it? No. But will you not maintain it? You will. This is how you should see it.

D: OK. You also tell us to not identify with the body. To not take myself to be an individual. Without being an individual how can I experience the love for her? Where is this love arising from?

Mahaprabu: Just to make you understand, let us look at it this way. Say: A = Atma; B = Vasanas i.e. mental depositions that are accumulated through various experiences over many births. C = Body; D = In this birth, the idea of me as a person, which is a memory deposition.

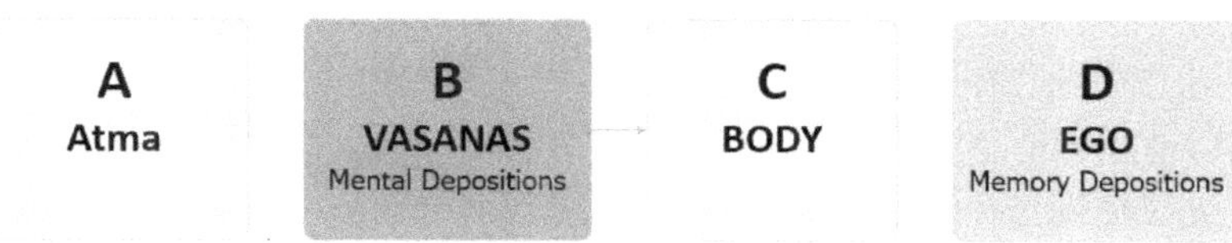

D: Then isn't the love arising from D, the idea of a person? So, unless I am an individual how can I experience it?

Mahaprabu: You have to make a choice. Be in Category One: My only priority in life is to attain Jnana. Whatever I get or not get, enjoy or not, I must attain Jnana. (or) Be in Category Two: I want Jnana and I want the other things too. Say Jnana is X, and various desires are Y1, Y2, Y3. If a seeker in category One comes to me, then I will handle him in a way that he doesn't get pulled into Y1, Y2, Y3. But if a disciple comes to me in category Two, then the energy has to be split between X and his Y's. Therefore there will be a delay in his growth. Till the point of tiredness of Y1, Y2 etc. I have to wait. So, you have to be clear about which category you are in. And if you are in Category Two, you should not talk like someone who is in Category One. (Laughing. Referring to the relationship he is thinking about) Be clear. First tell me which category you are in.

D: I'm in Category Two.

Mahaprabu: Then I will start talking to a Category Two person. But even if I talk in terms of Category Two, since eventually after Y1, Y2 etc are gone, my words will eventually turn towards X (Jnana), therefore it will sound to you like I'm talking to Category One person.

See, the love (desire for the lover) comes from B (Vasanas). See, B has Pleasure records but also has Pain records. What D (idea of individual) does is that it magnifies the Pain more than the Pleasure. That is why we suffer. *It is like seeing a small stone with a magnifying lens without knowing that there is a lens.* This is why most of our so-called problems appear larger than they actually are. This is because Pain records are always magnified more than Pleasure. That is how it is. So, we need to remove that Lens.

Let us go deeper. B has both Pain and Pleasure. To you it appears as two different things, but really they are not. It is like Brightness and Darkness. Even though they appear as different things, they are two extremes of one aspect, Light. Similarly, Likes and Dislikes, Pain and Pleasure seem to be two different things but they are extremes of one aspect. So if you go deep into B, Pain and Pleasure are one and the same. I cannot explain this further in words. You have to experience it at that depth. It is like this. *Say you are in Love. Now your task is to explain that feeling of Love to a small child. What will you say?* You cannot express it. It has to be experienced.

Now if you go below B and see who this Like and Dislike is for? It is for Atma A in the end. Which is the one with life here? Only Atma. So because of A, there is B. And because of B, there is C (body is born). Don't your records make you take birth accordingly? And due to C, the idea of person D is born (body identification).

D: So how can one be without D? If having a body means you have D, how can you be without it? I see a girl and think she is my lover. Only if I have D, I will feel her.

Mahaprabu: Your first question. Can I be without D. See, this A, B, and C is an integrated system. They cannot be avoided. But D is not part of it. For example, when you were a child in your mother's womb, was A there? Yes. Was the body C there? Yes. If A and C are there, then B definitely must have been there. You may not have felt it since it was a seed, but B is the cause for C. So, A, B, and C were there but was there D? No. And even after you came out into the world, D was not there. D comes later when people start identifying you as a male, with a name, etc. So what is D? A thought in the brain that has come from outside. Therefore D is related to what? Since the brain is part of the body, D is related to C. Now C is connected with what? B, its cause, stemming from A. So if D is connected with C and C is connected with A, then D is also indirectly connected with A. One by one you have to come out of this.

Who are you? You are actually A, but you are thinking you are D. The Atma A is thinking that itself is D. This is Ignorance. So if there is something you can remove now, it is D.

D: So should I keep reminding myself that I am not D, I am not D, I will not use this lens?

Mahaprabu: If you are able to do it, go ahead.

D: So when I am with this girl, and I practice this, when I look closely at D, I will lose D at that point. Then I feel the consciousness and am without D.

Mahaprabu: Yes, and when that happens how does it feel? Is that a disturbed state, something that you wouldn't want?

D: No. It actually feels peaceful.

Mahaprabu: Then what is the need for the love and the girl at that point (Laughing!!!). See how we fall into the trap of seeking happiness outside. Who is the one making you go outside? Your records B, which come out through D. So even though you say 'hypothetically when I am without D I would not be disturbed', you have not tried it. Remember that B is still there underneath. The Likes and Dislikes are still there. Only D is gone. B is still there. So, B will dominate and come out.

SC (disciple of Mahaprabu): So, B can operate without D through the body C?

Mahaprabu: Definitely. Don't children have likes and dislikes? They go towards some things, some people, and not others. Also doesn't an ant or bug have a body (C) without ego (D)?

The question is, without a Lover how can there be Love? Which is the Lover? D (ego). And Love? B (Likes and Dislikes). So without D, there can still be B. Remember this is not actually Love, but a desire. Where does this desire originate from? B or A.

SC: It is a deposit in B but must come from A.

Mahaprabu: It comes from A originally but is Reflected in B. From this love in A, comes a desire in B and is exposed as a sexual feeling which is experienced in C, the body. It is this combination of A, B and C that is responsible for creation. And D forms opinions about this, that 'If I indulge in desires, sex etc, there is a feeling of happiness'. It remembers these. For this it magnifies B. This is so it can continue in the next birth. (SC: Oh my God!) This capacity of D is more pronounced in humans only because of our advanced brain. See, an Amoeba or Ant doesn't have a brain. Then a very basic brain is formed. Dogs, Cats, Lions have a brain. Yet a Lion does not think I am a Lion (no D). But where are its records stored? In B. So D is not a requirement of B. B can be formed without D. But D magnifies, boosts, and strengthens B. For what? For the next birth!

SC: Wow! What a rascal.

Mahaprabu: Laughing. See the depth.

D: Oh Mahaprabu, I have so many problems.

Mahaprabu: So back to the main topic. You are in Category Two. B and D combined are bothering you. Actually, You don't exist. The problem is not for You. A exists, B exists, C exists. D is the one that has the problem. C won't even know if it has a problem (physical mass). A has no problem whatsoever. B is in between. So, don't confuse yourself with D. Strength is needed. Being more and more in Satsang and with the Guru will give you the strength. Be clear as to what is driving your love for the girl. Is it love or sex? See carefully.

Peace and Confusion.

Mahaprabu to D: Now, at this moment how are you feeling? You were so confused when you started.

D: I feel at peace.

Mahaprabu: That peace did I give you or was it there in you?

D: It was in me.

Mahaprabu: So, the confusion came from where? From you. That peace is there at the depth. The confusion is entirely on the surface only. Now you were able to go from that confusion to the peace. But you are swimming on the surface all the time. It has to be skipped entirely. You have to jump away from it. But what are all of you doing? Being in the state of confusion, you are trying to be without confusion, searching for a place without confusion. You are trying to find the solution while staying in the problem. When you are in confusion, when you search, you will only see what? Confusion. The key is to totally skip the confusion, and jump away from it. Only then you can be in peace. For a few seconds I was able to make you jump. But I am there in that state 24×7. Only a Jnani can do this. Only he has the capacity, the force to make you jump from Confusion to Peace. (*Kozappamana nilai lendhu kozappam atra nilai ku konduvara atral*).

So, see where you have to be and where you are right now. Who you have to be with. I am asking you to come to a place of no confusion (meaning with Mahaprabu). Instead you are wallowing in the state of confusion and suffering so much and giving up. But instead, as you stay with Mahaprabu longer, you will be more and more in a confusion-less state and it will become *sagajam* (natural) one day.

Only when you see Confusion from a confusion-less state you will find a solution to it. For example, say someone has a problem. You don't have that problem. Only you can see his problem objectively. Similarly, a person at times is in a confused state and there are times when he is clear. Only from the clear state when he sees confusion can he solve the confusion. What will remain? The unconfused state. As you continue to stay in the unconfused state, even though sometimes a confusion arises, you will see it for what it is. Just a confusion. You will skip it. The confused state goes away. What remains is again the unconfused clear state. One day all the states will be unconfused, clear. That is the Master. That is why anytime the disciple comes to the Master with confusion, his confusion soon becomes cleared easily. (SC has seen this happen so many times.) Because he sees the problem from a state of clarity.

But that is not the solution for you. You yourself should find that. You should become a master of coming out of confusion at all times. The intention of the Master is not for the disciple to follow him always. The intention of the Master is that the disciple should BECOME the Master. You should become the Master. Master of what? You should be able to manage all situations by seeing them from an unconfused state at all times. And when a new confusion occurs (due to traces of B or D), if you are able to jump out of it immediately and see it from the unconfused state then you will remain in peace. So developing this ability to jump from confusion to an unconfused state, seeing the problem, finding the solution objectively, and the confusion goes away, peace remains; and repeating it again and again till you remain unshakeable in the unconfused state, is the goal. This is what I call growth. And once you are established in that unconfused state permanently, there is no more growth since that unconfused state was already there, always there. Now there is no question of growth or depreciation. A Jnani speaks from there experientially. But so many teachers merely talk about this.

SC: So, the greatest achievement is to be able to remain in this unconfused state. Not knowledge or anything. None of that is necessary.

Mahaprabu: No question. It is the greatest Blessing. You have to move very fast towards this. Very fast you have to come to this. Don't get caught anywhere else. Who is today is gone tomorrow. Saying 'I will live for them', 'I will live for him', 'What will they think', is very dangerous. Once you see it in the unconfused state you will see them clearly. Decisions will become easy. It doesn't mean that it will be right every time. It may not be perfect at all times. Like Osho says: 'You cannot say that Jnanis will do everything perfectly at all times, but whatever they do will be perfect for that situation.' His actions will fit perfectly with the flow.

That's why I am saying 'Please, please run away from all this.' Because 50 years from now you won't have any idea who they are, where they are. In your previous life you were with a whole other group. Even now, tell me if you remember how you were in 5th standard. Or as a child. You can't even remember this birth. Take the father of your body. At his deathbed, when all the faculties fail, he won't even remember you. When you go to him and say 'Dad, I have come' he might say 'Who are you?' Because memory fades. It is all memory. Don't be cheated. Your entire world and all your relations are stored where? In your Brain. Even if all those memories turn off, Unarvu, Life, A will be there. C body will be there. Deposits B will be there. But D won't be there. Then C will go away one day. At that time, B will stick with A and stay. Then B will create another C. The next C. As long as B is there, C has to come. And if C comes, D will eventually come. With every birth B only has a higher chance of getting stronger and stronger. This world, things, these so-called relations, will all make D strong and through that make B stronger. Only the Guru makes D weak and through that makes B weak. All other relationships make D stronger, thereby making B stronger. Living with the Guru alone is strength. Only that gives you strength. Everything else sucks the strength away. See, even though you know what to do, you are not able to do it. Why? Because there is no strength.

Know that, which once you know, there is no need to know anything else. That IS inside.

So what Mahaprabu is saying is this: Do you know what you need? That which is there when you (D) disappear. You like that experience. All do. In sleep when you disappear, you enjoy that experience. This yearning for that is common for ALL. That's why more than sleep, sex is more vibrant. Sleep drags you away into losing you. The disappearance is in darkness. In sex you disappear but are still aware of the experience. It is happening consciously. That's why everyone likes it. Why? Because when you disappear, you are able to experience THAT which is there in your absence. In *Atma Anubavam*, the experience of Atma, the difference is that D disappears and A remains without B and therefore without the need for C.

It all comes down to bringing your attention inward and seeing what is real and what is not real.

Getting rid of B (Vasanas)

When Unarvu Nilai Dhyanam (a practice that comes from Mahaprabu at times, which puts us in touch with our existence) comes, depending on the maturity of the disciple it hits him directly. It can take you directly to A. But B quickly comes in the way. So without totally getting rid of B, there is no use.

SC: How to get rid of B?

Mahaprabu: Surrender is the only way. At one stage B happened without D. But once D came in, D started zooming it and strengthening it. So once you eliminate D, B won't have strength. It won't be zoomed.

SC: How about the deposits in B over many lifetimes?

Mahaprabu: That is not a big problem. As you keep on staying in Surrender those will come out. First D surrenders. Along with it, C also will be in surrender. D gets cut. Now A, B, C are left. But Surrender has to continue. Who started the Surrender? D. But D is gone. Yet Surrender has to continue, right? Can C do it? No. C has no *arivu* (feeling of its existence). C is *jada* (inert). Neither does B. B is mental structures. So, something has to surrender B & C. D used to do it. Now A (*Atma*) does that. So A itself will Surrender. That is *pari-poorana-saranagathi* (Total unconditional surrender).

SC: To whom?

Mahaprabu: To the Guru! That's who D surrendered to. A will also surrender. Slowly B will go away. Because B was formed without D, due to the connection with C. When B and C disappear, A will stand alone, pure. Once this happens totally, only then A will feel A. It would have felt it thus far as coming from the Guru, but eventually will realize that it is coming from itself. So without A getting involved, A cannot realize A. Right? How can A realize without involving itself? To realize A, A should be there, right? So, the Guru is just the mirror.

SC: Right now it feels like D is surrendering to the A in me. And I feel that A in me and the Guru are one and the same.

Mahaprabu: You should not go that way now. It is dangerous. Don't fall for the tricks of D. It will play treacherous games and will use B. Surrender only to the GURU.

SC: Physical form of Guru?

Mahaprabu: Better than physical form, say 'External'. (as opposed to your internal). It can be physical when you are with him, it can be mental when you are physically away. It can be a feeling. Like right now when you think of your father in India, is it physical?

Don't think that your Atma and Guru are one. Bhagavan said, '*Advaitam* (non-duality) can be practised anywhere in the 3 worlds but never with the Guru.' Using your brain alone you are guessing that your Atma and Guru are one and the same (Laughing). Many have been misled at this stage. There used to be a disciple, a really good Atma. At the time when he met Mahaprabu the body age was around 50 already then. He told me about his strong feeling that he had this question: Whether he should surrender to the Atma within, since he finds that to be even better than surrendering to a Guru. Mahaprabu could see that even though he was good soul, he was being pulled into a different track by the people around him. Mahaprabu told him that he definitely needed to surrender to the physical Guru, live with him and serve him. As you do that, at one point there will be a maturity. At that point, this question will not even exist in you. Right now you have a question, correct? That itself shows that there is no surrender, and that there is someone who is asking the question. For example, *having eaten well, if you are full, will you ask someone if your hunger has gone! No. You will know for sure yourself.* This disciple spent very little time with Mahaprabu and I noticed that he would become silent very quickly. But he did not listen and stuck to his other group. They were more interested in going on pilgrimages like trips to the Himalayas etc. He never came back to Mahaprabu again. See how one's own ego makes one lose a great opportunity.

SC: But really what I meant was that I strongly feel that there is something inside. If I had to give this feeling a name, I would call it God. I feel a strong sense of gratitude to it. It is the same feeling that happens when you give *Unarvu Nilai Dhyanam.*

Mahaprabu: That is OK, let it be. Yes there is God inside. But above that is B. And above that is D. Correct? So yes, there is definitely God inside, but when you say that there is God inside, do you know who is saying that? A or D or B. You don't. Until D and B are gone, don't give any definition to that. Enjoy it when it happens but do not give any definition or derivation. Do not go to any decision. Who is giving the definition? A or B or D?

SC: Only D would do that!

Mahaprabu: See! Be careful. Enjoy whatever comes at that moment. One thing to remember is as long as D is there, B will be there. Even after the disappearance of D, B will still be there. Correct? Till B completely disappears, till then the Surrender process of A should be continued. Surrender is the only way. Right now the Surrender is D's! I won't believe that surrender! Right now, Surrender is merely a decision. A decision by D. When A surrenders (which is the real Surrender) it will not be a decision. It will be a strong determination. A decision can be changed easily. But a strong determination cannot be revoked that easily. It is like a one-way process. It will move straight towards IT and finish it off. It is like this:

Before marriage, the girl (in Indian traditional arranged marriages) can evaluate and decide between various proposals. She can change her decision anytime. Even if the engagement function is complete, she can withdraw. But once the marriage happens can she easily withdraw? No. If they have entered into a physical relationship, even harder. Once they have children, the chances of her wanting to withdraw are very remote. The underlying determination will be very strong. Like that, as long as D is there, anytime it can withdraw from its Surrender. But when it reaches A, it is very hard to withdraw.

All this has to be experienced, not understood. Because these things happen in the absence of D. That's why it takes time. And people don't want to surrender. That's why people prefer a dead Master than a head Master. Because there is no problem at all with a dead Master. D inside the disciple decides the surrender and it stops there. It can keep making you believe that you are in surrender, when you are really not (since D and B are still intact). But with a real Master, he will demand the surrender of A! A dead master will not demand anything. The surrender and its boundaries are set by D. But with a real Master, the A in the Master is deciding the boundary of your surrender. That's why there is a difference. And it is a very big difference.

Great things are happening. We are on the right track. We just have to stick to it and let the process do its thing. The raw materials have arrived. The manufacturing process had begun. Your mindset should be this. That you have arrived. More than this there is nothing to be learned or understood from the Guru. Be in Surrender. This is an inner relationship. Not a knowledge transfer. The process has to happen. Like *we have planted a seed. It has to grow and come up to be the plant. You have to wait. And while waiting, the process is happening below. You don't start digging every once in a while, to see if the growth is happening!* (Laughing). [SC was Amazed at his apt examples.] *You will never let it grow, correct?* What is needed is tremendous patience.

Sacrifice everything for this

Every day you get is so important, a blessing. One has to use ALL his resources. Nature is giving it to you so you can use it. Time, Effort, Money, Enthusiasm all must be used. Say you have a thousand crore rupees. You used all of it towards your goal of Jnana and it got depleted to zero. But you have attained Jnana. Now you are a smart person. But on the other hand, if you have not used most of that money but died without attaining Jnana? That money will be here. But it was given for you to use. This is just money. Like that, Time has been given to you. The one who uses all or most of it to attain Jnana is an intelligent person. He who has wasted it is a fool. Similarly the Guru must be used to the maximum. All disciples need to realize this and work hard towards the goal. Every day is important. Look at Mahaprabu. The wife is in Chennai. Children are there. It is raining heavily. Still he is on the road heading towards Tiruvannamalai. For whom? For the disciple. Every minute is being used to move the disciples towards Jnana.

How to see relations

SC: (Amazed at his ability to separate, disconnect from family etc. even during his Sadhana period and remarked about it.)

Mahaprabu: Family is ignorance. What do we need? Our true nature is all we need. The lies have to go. Family is a lie. Yes, there are physical bodies. The Jiva that gave birth to this body (referring to the mother role). There is love for that Jivan because she took so much care of this body. That Jiva needs to be helped when there is a real need and when no one else is there to take care of it. That we should do. That is real. But that 'she' is a mother and that 'I' am a son is not true. It is imagination. What you are calling separation, disconnection is this: The lie, the possessiveness has been disconnected. But the Love is there, the blessing is there. And there isn't a real need on their end. Physically or for Jnana. If they had a need for Jnana, then I would relate to them but only as a Master–Disciple. Not as a mother. See again it is a matter of need. Not right/wrong. If she were a disciple, and there was another disciple who is younger but more mature spiritually, I would ask her (mother) to serve that younger disciple. It is not a matter of age but stage! So, even if she connects back, it will only be as a Master–Disciple, not Mother–Son. She will have to forget that she is a mother and I am a son, because that is not real. I have disconnected the possessiveness, the misconception but not the Love. That is why they are surprised (Mahaprabu's parents). They feel: 'We have been angry with him most of the time since he left us, but he has always showered only love on us'. SC asked how they know you shower love on them. Mahaprabu: Because I call them once in a while. I even visit them. When they really feel like seeing me, I go. Not as family. But out of gratitude. Love. They have not harmed me. Because they did not know the path I was in, they acted that way. They didn't support me, but they did not stop me. They feel that Love. For instance, the love they see from my siblings' body is mixed with expectation. But Mahaprabu's Love is different. There is no expectation. I hug and kiss them. Because I see them only as Atma which has not realized that it is Atma and is imagining it to be mother, father. A blessing goes from me to them when I see them, when I kiss them. Instead of them blessing me, the blessing goes from here. For them to receive that blessing IT sends me there! Either the Mohammedan should move to the mountain or the mountain should move to the Mohammedan!

I am a flow.

If they become the reservoir, the flow will happen. This holds good for anybody. If you become a reservoir, I am the flow. I am nothing but a flow. For instance, see how long we have been talking. More than one and a half hours.

Silence for some time. Then he said_.

A very big treasure of Jnana is sitting here in Mahaprabu. Suited for this stage of the world. A treasure that is suited to be accessible by this stage of the world.

———— ◆ ◄◄ ◈ ►► ◆ ————

August 27th, 2022
Rest House at Paliapattu

Boss and the Servant - 1

It was late in the night. We were having black coffee, which Mahaprabu brought as usual! What was delivered in the next hour or so was clarity at its best. Sri Mahaprabu went into great depths about how the system in us works, who is really in control and what our role, if any is. And he did it by sharing his own experience from a young age.

SC: You stress the importance of being aware of the feeling of existence moment to moment (*Unarvin thodarbu*). But it is not something that is commonly stressed by many Jnanis. Something like Zen seems to stress this more. Why is that? Mahaprabu started talking in depth about his experience.

Mahaprabu: I don't know anything. I don't know Zen. I don't know Patanjali. Nothing I know (referring to prior enlightenment).

SC: But how did this need to be in *Unarvin thodarbu* arise in you?

Mahaprabu: It came. Only one thing I found in me. I am able to feel that I was receiving some commands, some instructions from inside, beyond my control and based on those instructions I am acting. This I realized first. This was the Starting Point. On many occasions I was able to observe that some kind of instruction is coming from inside and based on those instructions given by something which is inside, I am acting. I don't know if by following that instruction I will get a benefit or not. It may lead to a good path or a bad path I don't know. But from the time I came out of childhood, when I started to know things, from then onwards I felt this. Except when sleeping, some voice inside me is giving instructions and I am following that.

SC: Even for trivial tasks?

Mahaprabu: Yes, for everything. Another thing I observed is that EVERYONE is functioning this way too. Some instructions are coming from inside. Attending to these instructions is how everyone is functioning. This is how the whole system is functioning.

The second thing I observed is that even if I want to be peaceful, i.e. stay quiet without thinking, something still keeps thinking. These are the two things that came to my attention from a young age.

I should be the Boss. If I am the Boss, I should think whenever I need thinking and whenever I don't need to think, the thinking should stop. If I am the Boss I have to be in control and function according to those decisions. But based on my observation some instructions are coming and I am following them and based on that I am functioning. If so, I am not the Boss. Whether I was the Boss to me or not? This was the very first question that came to me. Not devotion, not anything else.

This is how it is happening to all, but the difference between me and others is that I am taking this up as something important. Others are not giving importance to this. Everyone is thinking 'they' are giving the command and 'they' are executing it. But for me, I felt I was a separate person. In fact I strongly believed I was a person. I was the owner of the body. I am the hero of my own journey. But in spite of that, beyond me, so many instructions are coming. The decisions are not taken by me. Before I even think it gives me something and says, 'Do it.' Then I do it.

And what I found is that when IT makes a decision, the energy and power is much greater compared to when I think and make a decision.

SC: Please give me an example.

Mahaprabu: So many examples. If I see a girl and think that she is attractive, then I am able to feel that as a person I am thinking about the girl. I am the owner of this thinking. When I am the owner, I am able to feel the less amount of energy behind that thought. I know this is my own thinking. Yes, she looks nice, she is well-dressed. But there is no power behind that thought. I am not able to feel an energy. On the other hand, when I am not paying attention to a girl, say I am in a bus and accidentally I see this girl crossing. At that point, as a person I am not starting any thinking process. But some kind of thinking is coming inside me with tremendous energy which I have not felt when I was thinking of a person on my own. Like this in every occasion it would happen. For example, there is some money on the ground. I think, someone left it there. Poor man he must be suffering. I should give it to the owner. These thoughts have no force, no energy behind them. Or I might think, 'The money is like paper.' For these thoughts I am the owner, I can feel it. I can feel the lack of energy behind them.

Like this in so many instances I would observe the difference. So, who is the Boss? I am not the Boss. If I am not the Boss, then who is the Boss? I am thinking that this person (pointing to the body) is the Boss. But I am weak, not strong. And I can see somebody coming with energy, which I cannot match. That's when I realized there is something powerful inside, where these commands are coming from.

I decided one thing: One hour we will sit. A strong oath was taken. For 1 hour I should not talk about anything with me. Here 'I' refers to the 'person'. This was a tremendously strong decision. And once I implement this, if still thoughts are generated (if I didn't generate them), it means they are being generated somehow inside me. Which means I am able to find two people. One is me, who is clear that I won't think. I was honest about that decision. I knew that having made the decision I will not think for sure. So, if I was the single Boss, then no thoughts should come. If thoughts came, then someone else is the Boss. This was where my journey started. Instead of Bhagavan's 'Who Am I', the question to me was: Who is the Boss inside? How is he? Does he have a form, or a colour? All these days have I not seen him?

Like this the investigation continued. Then after a point the Boss was no longer important to me. What mattered was the place where the thoughts came from. The Boss was only an idea. Somebody is commanding. That was the issue. Not the idea of a Boss. Then I began to focus like a laser on that Source where thoughts were coming from. As the focus became deeper and deeper and even more deep, I disappeared. Some inner system is there, and I am there as a person turning my attention towards it. This is my job now.

As this continued for a long time, I understood that there are two things: An inner system and the Brain. The inner system is the Boss. The Brain is the Servant. That's all the Brain is. That's why he has less energy. Because it is a dummy. It is an instrument. It can observe whatever is happening. That's all. The Servant can observe what the Boss is doing, and the Servant can never become the Boss. That's all.

This practice continued at great depths very often during the day. I would go deeper and deeper towards the source of the commands (the Boss) and disappear. I could feel that I was moving towards the location, but not the location. Moving towards the location alone was in my hands, and at one point that which was moving also disappeared. What was moving towards the location? It was the brain. So at some point the brain that was going towards the location, that brain itself disappears.

But I knew that the location, that source of commands should have still been there. It wouldn't have disappeared just because the brain disappeared. The brain was not exposed to it. This made me think 'OK, I should keep moving towards the source, but I should not disappear, I should not disappear. This needs more alertness.' Later I found out why the brain was disappearing. It was exactly like sleep. When you lie down to sleep, the brain thinks about various things. The brain is working but slower and slower. At one point the brain stops. Then we are happy. We don't care about where the brain went etc. We happily sleep. This is happening every day. And now in the name of *dhyanam* what am I doing? With the same brain, I am searching for this location. And while searching it disappears. So what is happening is that the Brain is going to sleep just like it does at night. After some time I would wake up. I was searching for something but disappeared on the way. How will I ever find it?

When I realized it was sleep that was making me disappear, my goal became 'I should not sleep'. This is *villipu unarvu*. This is Awareness. I became more alert. Total attention of the brain was there while watching. There was a total focus on the Source. I, the brain did not even move toward IT anymore. The brain just stayed there. Sleep was just an aspect of the brain. So really nothing was going towards and nothing was disappearing. i.e. the Brain was always there. It did not move and it did not disappear. Sleep was just a modification in the brain. Because of that modification, it appeared as though I went in and disappeared.

Now the brain was totally alert and watching. Something beyond the body which does not have any muscles, IT comes. IT occupies. IT speaks. IT feels. IT moves. IT wants. IT occupies. (While speaking these words, his tone and voice softened considerably. And he instantly went into Samadhi as we have seen many, many, many times. After a while he resumed. And as always, he resumes amazingly exactly where he left off).

The Boss

Mahaprabu: A person thinking as a person, records information about a person having disappeared. It is a mere record in the brain. Once the brain realizes who is the real Boss, it no longer is interested in recording what the person is doing. **This is how personhood goes away.** The centre which is nameless, formless, independent of time and space and doesn't have any limits, this centre is the Boss. It is living, it is going, it is coming. Coming and going is only determined by the movement of the body but actually there is a stillness. In that angle it is not going it is not coming. It is living.

No more confusion in the brain. No two. Only one. IT is the owner. It has every right to use all parts of the body INCLUDING THE BRAIN. The brain understands this and drops personhood. No more two.

As long as there are two, due to that duality, that separation, everything will appear as two extremes. That is why everyone is able to feel happiness and suffering. Actually there is only one thing. How can you find suffering in happiness? You can't. Either there should be suffering or happiness. If there was only suffering, it cannot include happiness. And vice-versa.

SC: But we attribute that to time. An hour ago I was happy. Now I am suffering.

Mahaprabu: That's what. Because there is duality you feel that way. Whenever the Boss is coming out, he feels joy. Whenever this personhood comes, and things don't happen according to its wishes, it feels like it is suffering.

SC: This disappearance of joy is called suffering.

Mahaprabu: Yes. You are not suffering actually. Not experiencing joy does not mean there is suffering, but you are defining that there is suffering. So where is this part called Suffering?

SC: It is in the brain.

Mahaprabu: So is there any real suffering?

SC: My God. There isn't.

Mahaprabu: Yes. Suffering is where?

SC: Just an idea!! (At this point Mahaprabu began laughing for some time...)

This is what I have been saying all this time. How can there be two things? The definition you have given to suffering is wrong. Can joy become absent? No. It is a permanent one. How can a permanent one become absent? Your brain was not able to see the presence of the joy. It defines that as 'Joy is absent'. The Joy is not absent. The fact that the Brain did not focus on it, makes the Brain to believe, to say that Joy is absent. This is purely a confusion. Once this confusion is clearly understood and gone, then it is over.

SC: Wow it is just an idea. It's like there is light everywhere, but I close my eyes and say there is this thing called darkness, and I suffer it.

Mahaprabu: Yes. Now, where did we start this discussion: You asked why so many *jnanis* don't speak about this moment-to-moment Awareness. They say different things. Not many focus on *Unarvin Thodarbu*. The reason I told you all this now, is to show you how I reached here. This is how I sat and did this.

So, where is the clarity needed? Deep in your brain. There is no problem in Existence. It always IS. The confusion is in the brain. Whether your brain gets cleared of the confusion or not, does Existence care? It lives on.

SC: Then when you stress devotion, what do you mean in terms of the Boss and Servant? Does it mean that the brain is submitting to the Boss?

Mahaprabu: If you truly realize that you are the Servant and that there is a Boss, what would you do? You will start doing whatever the Boss says. You will start sweeping, cleaning etc. You will be in Surrender. There won't be any confusion about whether you are a Servant or a Boss anymore. You are the Servant he is the Boss. But now you have a confusion. Sometimes you are feeling like you are the Boss. Other times you feel like a Servant. See how funny. The Servant himself is confused about whether he is the Servant of the Boss. The Boss will never have this confusion. It is the Servant who is confused! (laughing)

SC: So looking back... in your case, the one that put all this effort in the first place, the effort to find all this, that's the brain too correct?

Mahaprabu: Definitely. Does the Boss need any effort? Confusion is where? In the brain. Who is suffering? The brain. So who wants the remedy? The brain. Who will put the effort toward that remedy? The brain.

SC: But then the thought to do all this research came from the brain too. Therefore it would not have had that much energy (compared to the instructions coming from IT.)

Mahaprabu: That's why I told you, I had to sit for hours and hours for a long part of my life. Sitting was my profession. (Long silence)

This whole thing is a confusion

Once the personhood record goes from the brain, there is crystal clarity in the brain. Everything becomes clear. What is the source of the confusion? The record that you are a person. Which makes you think that you are the Boss. You have no doubt at all that you aren't the Boss. But the Boss is somebody different!! When you don't have any doubt how would you even know to search for a Boss? 'I am the Boss' is your basis. It is the record that makes you think you are the Boss. So that record has to be cleared. This is why the first instruction of Mahaprabu's teaching is *Nabarthanmayin adipadayil seyal paduvadhai muzhuvadhumaaga vittu pazagudhal*. Getting used to performing all actions without the idea of a person.

Till that record is there, the thinking process goes on like it is the Boss. So it never cares or knows about the real Boss. And the real Boss continues to live. Due to that duality, You are absent to the Joy. The presence of the Brain, the attention of the Brain is not on the Joy. But it is searching for Joy. Because it is thinking that we are not in the joyful state. That's why it keeps searching. Because the Boss is Joy. And the taste of Joy also was recorded in the Brain by the Boss (Laughing).

So this entire thing is a confusion, a malfunction that happened in the brain. This is the real disorder. When this clears, the brain will be a muscular brain. It will not be a Boss. It will not take thinking into its hands. It will turn off. Now the Boss will come freely, 24×7. He will come into the brain and use it when needed, like using the eyes, using the nose. As the Boss has his own freedom, he may come at any time to the brain. And he may not come. Then the brain will be turned off to thinking. Then there is no rush or urgency (*padattam*) at all. Why is there no *padattam*? Because there is always a joyful state here (pointing to the heart). So there is no need to search for it outside. Even now when you seek joy outside, e.g. eating a bun-butter-jam (a common delicacy here), an external object you are really kindling the joy inside. You don't know that. But I know very clearly that the joy is not there. I am the joy. It is a bun, flour, a physical substance.

SC: When you say 'I' who are you referring to?

Mahaprabu: The Boss. I am the Boss. No confusion here. There is no Servant here.

SC: Brain is just like the eyes!

Mahaprabu: Yes, just like the fingers.

SC: When I try to observe 'Who is the thinker' at that point the one who is searching for the thinker disappears. It happens every time although am unable to stay that way for long. But when you searched, you compared your disappearance to sleep.

Mahaprabu: I was talking about how it was in me. That doesn't have to be the same with you. You just have to keep it up. When you disappear, stay there. Like Sadhu Om says, *Ninaipadhu yaar endraya ninaipadhu nindru pogum.* When you look at who is thinking, the thinking stops. *Ninaipilla podhum needhan irrupadhil ayyam undo.* There is no doubt that you exist, even when thinking stopped. *Nina pezum moolam idhil nilaypadhe nilayai nillu.* Stay in the source where thoughts originate.

If there was no Boss, no Existence, will the brain think? No. So *ninaipezum moolam*, the source from which the thoughts arise, refers to the Boss. *Nilaipadhe Nilayam Nillu* means 'Be the Boss.'

Now when you say 'I disappear, but am unable to stay that way for long', what is the reason? So far when we say brain, all the while we are talking about what? The memory depositions (Ego). Those can be cleared out of the way momentarily to give you some silence. But that is not total, nor does it last long. Because of the Mental Depositions (Vasanas). So, getting rid of the memory depositions (the idea of a person, D – refer to the Talk titled ABCD's for a great understanding of the fundamentals) alone is not enough.

SC: Even if D goes, B remains.

Mahaprabu: Yes. The Vasanas have to go too. When I went deep, I saw that too. (SC Amazed) Who was watching that too? The Brain. The Brain is keenly observing. At that time it is not playing its games. Totally alert. It sees that the Boss is unable to flow freely, due to these Vasanas. It found that the Boss itself is not free! The Boss is in prison. Due to the Vasanas. So just like there is a disorder here (pointing to head), there is a disorder here also (pointing to the heart). That disorder also has to be fixed. Only then that STILLNESS will prevail. Only then no matter what happens there will be a STILLNESS. Then you will feel a dynamic stillness. Inside sensitivity – Outside activity. A perfect Balance. This is called Zen. That will happen. Till then, the confusion will continue. The difference is that now the brain will wait. For its part, the brain won't add to the confusion. The brain will understand what is under. The brain will accept. It will wait. Even though the Boss is having his freedom he is in sickness. This is symbolized by the thorns around the heart when Jesus is depicted. So he should get cured. This curing has to happen.

SC: If the Boss himself is sick who can cure him?

Mahaprabu: God through the Master. That's why even though he is the Boss we say he is the Jiva and He is Siva. Siva himself has trapped himself in sickness and become a Jiva.

It is like this: *A bird can fly. It knows to fly. But it is in the cage. Just because it is in a cage, has it lost the ability to fly? No. Yet is it able to fly? No. This is just to* understand, so don't take it literally. The state of the Jiva is just like that bird.

SC: And the cage that we think we are in, is imaginary, correct? Our own creation?

Mahaprabu: No. It is not a mental creation. The cage in the example is iron bars. But here the cage is not imaginary. It is made of various sicknesses. Jealousy, tit-for-tat, greed, anger etc. Which can feel jealousness, the Brain (pointing to the head) or the Centre (pointing to the heart)?

SC: The centre.

Mahaprabu: Yes, the brain may kindle a thought that leads to the jealous feeling, but that feeling is not in the brain. It is deep in the mental depositions that have formed over several janmas, lifetimes.

How healing happens

Before the brain has attained clarity, a jealous thought created by the brain (who is the Servant thinking himself to be the Boss) will kindle the jealousness in the heart. The feel from there will merge with the thought in the brain and come out. In this way the brain helps the sickness to grow. This is how mental depositions get stronger. But once the brain gets clarity, that is, when the memory depositions in the brain go and those disorders are cleared, even though the mental depositions (vasanas) are there, now the brain will not support the sickness to grow further. Healing starts now. The brain helps the healing. Only now the brain starts to act like a Servant with devotion.

SC: All these negative emotions like Jealousy etc, come when we take ourselves to be a separate individual. Where did that first separation happen?

Mahaprabu: Laughing. In this total cinema, somewhere in the past, it slipped. Due to a lack of alertness. That's why if you are not careful, there is a good chance to go back. That is why a Jnani, even after enlightenment is very alert so it doesn't happen again. See, if it has happened once there is every chance for it to happen again, right?

What is needed is this. Clarity in the brain. Purity in the heart. Then there will be integrity. A wholeness. Without this wholeness, you feel sick mostly. You don't feel Joy a lot, correct? *It is like that bird continuously trying to fly in the cage, its wings are bruised and bleeding from the continuous effort to fly. Will it feel joy? And how can it enjoy flying? So, the cage has to be broken. Then when* *it flies, it will feel the joy of flying in the sky. The cage is not imaginary. It is real. It is a disease.* There comes devotion. The cure. The Boss has to beg. The bird has to cry for help so it can be released from the cage. Releasing the bird from the cage is the greatest help. It does not want any help with flying. It needs to come out of the cage. That is why Paramahamsa cries and cries so much.

SC: Who breaks the gate Mahaprabu?

Mahaprabu: You cry. That's all. Does the bird care who opens the cage? Does it matter? Don't take the example literally. When you cry the healing happens. One of the best healing medicines is *Omkaram* (Chanting Om for a long time several times a day). A great medicine for inner purification. I have not read this anywhere. It came automatically. When I went deep, I was able to find the sickness. I want to fly but am unable to. I wanted to fly but something is restricting it. I could feel the restriction. I started shouting. That shout created the sound Om. Om is the sound of the soul. In the beginning it is a *soga-ragam* (a sad raga) of the one who is sick. But as you shout it, chant it, again and again, it becomes a *suga-ragam*, a happy raga of the Om. Initially Om was an outlet. It comes on the way. Use it. I have not read anything. I sincerely, honestly went deep and kept going deep. Direct experience.

SC: Am amazed at your ability to observe your own system so sharply, that too from a young age. That is not the case here.

Mahaprabu: It will come. You are on the way. It cannot be avoided. Now don't measure and anticipate. It may come even tomorrow. And there is no rule that it should happen the same way for all. For example, *there may be 10 bands in the path (bandwidth). The frequency of each band will be different for each.* Because my vasanas can be totally different from yours. One may have a lot of vasanas around jealousy. For another, it might be totally absent, but he may have a strong Kama vasana. You need to go deep. The memory depositions have to go. That is in your hands. Then there are the mental depositions. With the Guru's help, when you are in total surrender, they can be destroyed. You don't analyze the vasanas. You stay in surrender. Analyzing and going into your vasanas will keep you trapped. *It is like the bird counting the number of rods in the cage, seeing what material they are made of, etc. None of this will help the bird come out of the cage. Even if the count is right!!*

Only when you feel trapped like a bird in a cage, this is possible. The first help of the Master is that he will make you realize that you are trapped in a cage. At the outset, you may not see that as a help, but actually it is a help. *Otherwise, you won't even know you are in a cage and keep flying inside thinking you are free. And everyone around you is pretending to fly in their cage, that it has become normal to be that way.*

Before meeting Mahaprabu and now, see how much your sitting practice has increased.

SC: Astronomically. I couldn't sit for even 5 minutes. Most time was spent in reading more, watching YouTube videos, thinking, and talking. Everything but sitting.

Mahaprabu: And right now I am only working part-time and you are far away physically. Soon this will change and I will enter into this full-time. So imagine how much more can happen.

A long silence followed.

September 30th, 2022
Around midnight, Sitthalapakkam House.

Boss and the Servant - 2

After a long stillness, even eating a sweet was with total detachment which resulted in a very different experience. On sharing this with Mahaprabu he dived into a close observation of what is happening. What is enjoyment, Who enjoys, Why and How. With that understanding, suffering is clearly seen as imaginative and unnecessary. Another must-read!

Mahaprabu: Whenever you and yours is absent, immediately at those times the silence will be felt.

[He said it in a certain deep tone with eyes closed as he drifted into Samadhi. Around 2 hours had passed in meditation sitting in front of Sri Mahaprabu. All track of time was lost. After coming out of Samadhi, he shared some Palkoa (a milk sweet) that he had brought. As we were eating it, I could sense a total detachment from the sweet, the resulting sensation and the person eating it and after some time mentioned this.]

Mahaprabu: Detached is a very correct word. One has to be detached. How is this detachment created? It is because of the Awareness. So being detached and being Aware is one and the same. If you are not Aware you are lost. And you become addicted to being a person. Now you are enjoying the sweet with Awareness. In this state is there anything wrong with the senses? No. (referring to the notion that the senses are dangerous and can drag you down.)

Enjoyment. By Whom, Why and How.

IT is enjoying. It has created the senses for that purpose. See it has created the sweet, created the tongue, and the taste buds on the tongue, all to enjoy its creations. And yet nothing, not even a small particle of the sweet will reach THAT. A part of the sweet may enter into the body, even to the cells. But it never touches THAT. Similarly, the taste in this sweet too does not reach THAT. Nothing reaches THAT. Yet there is a joy. By feeding the Palkoa to the body, it is kindling the joy in itself!

Palkoa is gross. Taste is subtle, but it is still in the gross body, in the taste buds, and brain. Neither of these reaches IT. Yet it has created everything just to enjoy, and kindle the joy already in it. (Laughing).

SC: While eating this tasty sweet, there is certainly enjoyment, there is a pleasure. So IT is enjoying that?

Mahaprabu: Yes, definitely. IT alone is enjoying it. But without knowing this, the brain thinks there is a person who is enjoying it. See there is a False centre (pointing to the head) and there is a True Centre (pointing to the heart). The Palkoa, a soft sweet is entering the body. The False centre and the True centre both recognize it. But where your recognition stops, is at the False centre. It doesn't come to your Awareness that the True centre is enjoying. You stay at the surface. Really IT (the Boss) is enjoying the experience. But the brain (the Servant) has forgotten that this is happening in the background. I will give you an example so you can see. *There is an owner of a very large estate with so many workers. A new worker has been appointed as a driver of the estate jeep. It is his first day at work. All the workers know their boss very well, but the new driver (the servant) has not seen him. The driver has been asked to pick up someone at the airport. (He has not been told that the person being picked up is the Boss, the owner of the estate). He brings the Boss to the estate. The Boss is sitting at the back of the Jeep. But the servant has forgotten that. He enjoys driving the jeep now imagining that he is the owner. As the jeep enters the estate, all the workers in the estate salute the BOSS (who is sitting in the back seat of the jeep). The SERVANT driving the jeep sees them saluting and believes they are all saluting him!!!!*

(Laughing). You see! The body, the entire system is like the workers in the estate. They know the real BOSS, the True centre. They have no confusion. But this SERVANT, the False centre, the idea of a Person also called the Ego, is the only one that thinks he is the Boss. In fact, he never questions that he is not the Boss.

So the experience of eating the sweet is not an imagination. It is happening. And the BOSS is actually enjoying it. But this SERVANT gets in the way and thinks HE is enjoying the sweet, and that his happiness comes from the sweet. (Laughing)

SC: Makes sense. Then why is it that beyond a point the very sweet becomes too much, we don't enjoy it?

Mahaprabu: Because the body becomes troubled by excess. Who owns the body? The Owner (the True Centre). He has created limits in the body. These external joys are *cittrinbam* – Little Pleasures. All sense pleasures are little pleasures for Him. In Samadhi is the real *perinbam* (Great Joy, Bliss). See how it limits how much you can put into the body at one time. It stops you.

But tomorrow you will resume liking the same sweet. This is natural. But the Servant can override it and result in over-feeding the body, resulting in negative consequences for the body. Like this, in many places the Boss says enough but the Servant who is addicted to sense pleasures wants to keep enjoying and suffers the consequences.

Notice how the enjoyment in eating the sweet with awareness and detachment is so different. It is not indulgence. It won't result in over-eating. Because IT is enjoying. And see how it has created a variety of things for its enjoyment. Imagine *you are extremely hungry. There is a lot of rice that has been cooked. But that's all there is. Half a kilo of just plain white rice. One taste only. Can you eat that plain rice beyond a point? Even though you are hungry you cannot. You might eat around 200 grams. Now, say there are other dishes to eat the rice with, such as vegetables, sambar, rasam, etc. Now you will eat a lot more rice. You will even finish the half kg of rice!*

See how it has created variety for its enjoyment. And even with that variety, it has set limits. Once your tank is full you are unable to eat. The Boss has set it all up correctly. It knows the Body needs energy. It knows the limits of the body as IT has set it. Why has it set limits? Because a) It does not want the body to get affected physically and b) It doesn't want the body to get tired of things. It has to eat food the next day!! *It is like you have been given a bank account with money. You can spend it all in a day. It is your freedom. But you will suffer for the rest of your life. So ideally you will spend a required amount each day.* That is how even sense pleasures have been set with limits.

This is how IT, the Atma keeps enjoying itself. It is always happy by nature. Yet it reminds itself of the joy, it rekindles that joy frequently. Without the Body also IT is ever blissful. With the body also IT kindles its own joy. Osho has beautifully captured this point when he said: First you be happy, then you can worry about Jnana. Why? Because happiness is ITS nature. The existence which is existing here and now is ever happy. It can exist with or without the body. Once it takes the body also, it tends to be happy. It cannot avoid happiness. That is how it is designed. But WE have entered (imaginary person) and say we should not indulge in pleasure, especially in the name of spirituality. That's why those who engage in those paths of extreme denials rarely succeed. Osho is referring to enjoyment with Awareness. This way you ensure that the body also is not affected, since you would not indulge.

The Right Understanding

Look, when you eat the sweet, it is going into the body. Then, who senses the taste? The body. So, who should be happy then?

SC: The body.

Mahaprabu: Yes, that is what is actually happening. By making the physical body happy, the Master behind that body is also enjoying it. Because the body is a servant to the Master. Good so far. But who is he that says "I am happy while eating this sweet?" An imaginary person! See how wrong the understanding is. So, when the same sweet is eaten with the right understanding, this enjoyment will not do any harm. But are we living with the right understanding? Forget about Atma Jnana. If you are present to what is happening moment to moment, you will be happy. The design is perfect. Just be in IT. So what needs to be fixed? The understanding, that's all. A wrong understanding has taken place. It needs to be corrected.

See carefully. Does Atma need Atma Jnanam? Only your Ajnanam (ignorance) needs Atma Jnanam (enlightenment).

And when will the right understanding happen? When Awareness is there. While eating the sweet if you think, it is over. 'Oh, what a taste. Where did you buy it.' etc. The minute you think, and then verbalize, you are not present. Then you are not in the flow. You don't feel the real joy.

Suffering is false and a waste

Even this understanding right now is happening for you in the brain. It is very likely that the Servant is doing the understanding! But after the meditation when you enjoyed the sweet, it was different. It was direct. When you are present moment to moment, you get a direct experience of everything. What IS Moment-to-Moment?

SC: Atma.

Mahaprabu: Then what should we do? Be there moment to moment. (Which really means the i becomes absent).

And if moment to moment only Atma is there? What is there moment to moment?

SC: Joy.

Mahaprabu: Yes. That's it. Only Joy will be there. Suffering will not be there, correct? So now see, is suffering real? No. It is imaginary. (Laughing). How can you suffer? Even if you try you cannot. It is imaginary. (Continued laughter from Mahaprabu). Is suffering your right understanding or wrong understanding!!! (Laughing).

When you live moment to moment, will you even talk about Suffering? Will you even talk about Atma? So besides living moment to moment, everything you do is a waste. Say you suffered a lot this morning. Is it useful or a waste? A total waste. All your suffering is a waste. How can you live with people in this world? Everyone believes they are suffering. Try telling them 'Suffering is not existent'. They will make you suffer!

As suffering is non-existent, Atma will not suffer even during the death of the body. It will be happy to get rid of this body and take on a new one. But the imaginary Servant suffers tremendously!! In fact, we are calling him Servant. That is a decent name. But what a treacherous thing this ego is. Buddha called it 'Kodunkhol Mannan' – An evil ruler, a tyrant! See which is the right definition. Servant or Evil Tyrant!

When you get a direct experience, any understanding in your brain will not stay, and won't be needed. But what everyone is doing, trying to cling onto so many understandings, thereby creating more opportunities for suffering.

Ok now that you know all this, when you still suffer, you will feel so bad. Because you will think, 'Oh God. Even after understanding it, I am still suffering.' So you have to develop the ability to jump out of it and come back to the moment. That ability to jump requires strength.

SC: So, IT has created everything for its enjoyment, including other people for it to interact?

Mahaprabu: Where is the question of 'other' people? How can I see you as 'other'? *It is like, in this room, the air is There and the air is Here. But can you say that is different air and this is different air? Two ends of a rope. One appears higher one end appears lower.* But is there really a difference? No. In reality there is no difference. Only the understanding needs to be corrected.

——————— ◆ ◂◂ ◈ ▸▸ ◆ ———————

October 5th, 2022
Well past midnight, Sithalapakkam House.

About Love

Most seekers come to the Master for knowledge. Instead, what is needed by them from the Master is Love. Why? Because that which we are seeking in the form of knowledge is actually Love. Sri Mahaprabu explains this step by step, along with what exactly a disciple needs to do, to realize his true nature.

Mahaprabu has seen this very clearly. When someone does something with love, for a Master, no matter what it is, no matter how small it is or how big it is, no matter who the person is, a small boy or an adult, when you do it with Love, THAT MATTERS.

It must be done with Love from your heart. For example, say the heart in front of me is filled with 10% love. Out of that some portion is conveyed to the master, then what is reciprocated is 100 times that. Just for your understanding. It comes back to you more than a hundred-fold. It echoes back multiplied. Take a basic task such as talking. Most of the time we talk from here (pointing to the head), where there is no love at all. 99% of people coming towards spirituality when they meet a Master, they are coming from here (pointing to the head). So, zero love comes towards the Master and therefore they in return receive nothing. Even if they had shown 1% love, they would have received a lot more in return. And what is it that benefits the disciple the most from a Jnani? It is Love. I have seen this very closely.

A Jnani is not a resource

But people mostly treat the Jnani as a resource. Once you treat something as a resource, you want to use it. You want to take it, obtain some benefit from it. You are in business now. A Master is not a resource. He is the Source. That's all. He is a Source for what? For your Wisdom. He is not a resource for your wisdom. When you start feeling that the Master is a source for your wisdom you will be a receiver. You will become empty. There will be surrender. There will be no attempt. Instead, if you think that the Master is a resource, there will always be an attempt. But initially most seekers reach a Master thinking that he is a resource. Still the Master accepts the seeker. He will simply come, have a conversation and go, then come again. Once he realizes that the Master is not a resource but the Source, then he starts to receive even without his knowing. There is a big difference between 'you will receive' vs. 'you will use.' In using, there is an ego. In receiving there isn't.

Love is the Receiver

So be a receiver. What is the receiver here? It is Love. You don't need knowledge. Knowledge is tied to the brain. Can the brain see Love? Is the brain the centre for Love? You can keep huge amounts of information in your brain. But as long as you are coming from the brain you will never get the real benefit from the Master. See, the Master wants to give Love. He never wants to give information. His intention is to make you feel the Love, thereby you can also come to know that there is a Source for Love. And that you are also the Source of Love. Until then Love is just information for you. L.O.V.E is not Love.

The Master knows that it is a waste of time as long as there is only an information exchange, but he still waits, to see if there is love arising. If the disciple stays at the information level, Love will only be a word in the brain. Just another piece of information. The brain will process it, and try to understand it like anything else. By processing Love, the brain cannot get Love because the brain is in no way connected with Love.

Feeling, not Words

You are also the Source of Love. What you have missed is feeling and experiencing the Love which is flowing, which is everywhere. That's why for many years in Satsang I did not allow the usage of the words Brahman, Atma, etc. Disciples should not use these words. Because when you say Atma, it is just a word in your brain, without an experience behind it. You have formed some knowledge about what is unknown. Don't speak about something you don't know. Don't give it a name. Let the unknown be unknown. Only then you will at least have the intent to know it. Once you have given it to your brain, anything you encounter will only strengthen that. You know what is even more funny? You are the real Atma, here and now. But you will be trying for the projected one! And you will try to convince the Master that you have reached the projected Atma!

On the other hand, you know what Love is. You have felt it. Of all the feelings in you, the one that lasts the longest the one that does not bore you, the one which you don't want to avoid – What feeling is that? It is only Love. Even with sex, people get bored with it and even avoid it after some time.

But Love is unique. It never gives a feeling that you should avoid it. It is unique. So, start there.

Do you know about Love? This Love – does it originate from the Brain? Have you created Love? No. But you know that it gives me a very good feeling. Its absence makes me unhappy. It is inside me. But it is not coming out in its full form. It is struggling to come out. If it came out unrestricted 24 hours a day, how would it be? Would I avoid it? No. 24 hours would you like to be angry? 24 hours have sex? No. See, only Love is that way. Then why is it not coming out?

Your efforts then must be what? To maximise the opportunity for the Love to flow. Actually, what is existing here and now, which is bodiless, independent of space and time, limitless, and endless is LOVE. As a source it is inexhaustible. As you cannot exhaust it, it is limitless. You know very well that you have not created this. What is Godliness? When you are filled with tremendous, overflowing love in you, that state is called Godliness. I am not talking about the word 'Godliness'. The name is not Godliness. God has not given the name. Someone who has felt that wonderful state in him has given it that name. That state of Godliness directly relates to Love. Can you differentiate Godliness and Love? Love in its original form is Godliness. *Rainwater is the original water. All other things are mixed. River water, Tap water etc.*

How to bring out the Love

How to bring out the Love in me? It is flowing naturally, but there are blocks. So, the efforts are not to create Love or to increase the Love. You have to remove the obstacles that are blocking it. Remove them and it will flow. How do you remove the blocks? Only by living with the Master, being in Surrender. When you interact with others, as the egos are interacting, there is no flow of love. But it is very easy to move and talk with a Master as he has no ego. He talks from the heart. He lives for you. Actually, a Master is the Servant Who Serves Those Who Deserve.

Love (Master) accepts everything. And vice versa. When there is acceptance, there is Love. Acceptance is the expression of Love. The other name for Acceptance is Surrender. Think. If there is no acceptance, can there be Love? That's why a Master keeps on stressing the importance of Acceptance. When you start accepting, you are preparing yourself to express Love. Why express Love? Because Love is God. What do you want to achieve through spirituality? You want to meet God, embrace God, and live with Him. Who is

God? God is Love. So, to meet him, you must have Love 100%; you must become Love itself. How? Through Acceptance and Surrender to a living Master.

Love and Awareness

Feeling and enjoying the flow of Love in its full form, realizing that what is existing is Love, is called enlightenment. And if you experience that Love, you will experience another thing along with it. Something makes me recognize that Love. You will realize that Love is a feeling with knowledge i.e., Awareness. The knower, known and knowing, all are one. The Knower is Love, the Known is Love and the process of knowing is also Love. It is very different from the Love you have recorded in your brain. Real Love is a continuous flow, with Awareness about itself. When we speak about Love, we forget Awareness. We use the word unconsciously.

Love (Anbu) and Awareness (Arivu) are not two different things. They are inseparable. That's why we give importance to Love. Where there is Love, the Awareness of its existence, Knowledge, will follow automatically as they are inseparable. But instead, seekers start from Arivu, from the brain. Finished! They break their head about so many things. Instead, you know about Love, you know you want it, and you know that everyone wants it. Start there.

In 2006 when Satsang started, I only spoke about Love. Only Vaiai Subramaniam (author of Yellam Ondre – All is One) touched on this. He says: Approach God with name and form. Be loving to him. Slowly your mind will mature. Then you will progress to higher levels. But even easier than this, there is a way. But when you hear it, you will think that it is a cheap one and you will not tend to follow it. But truly there is no easier way than this. It is the best way. That way is this: *Unnal nanmai adayavo theemai adayavo bhadhya pattula anaithu uyirgalukkum nee kattum anbu.*

Showing Love to all beings who are going to benefit from you or be hurt by you – That is the best way.

See the words. You will love someone you like, but imagine showing love to someone who is hurting you or even someone who is going to be hurt by you. Meaning, he is going to do wrong to you, or even when you are going to do wrong to him. In all cases show love. Always give importance to Love. That's what he is saying. This is the simplest and most direct route. But even he did not stress it. He did not make it his focal point. Yet he authorizes it.

The Master can show you the way to bring that Love out. Do that. Instead, people are feeding more and more information from outside and are breaking their heads over so many complicated things. Instead of the continuous flow of ego in you, keep on giving importance to the flow of Love in you. For this, you have to keep the flow of Awareness. Only when you are aware you will at least know if there is Love flowing or not. Once you are aware that the Love is not flowing, you can at least cry for it. That will lead you to it. Love knows about its existence.

When you are with the Master, he will easily show you where all your ego is flowing instead of Love. The disciple needs to be ready to bear that, accept that, feel sorry for it and rectify it. That flow in you should transform from 10% Love and 90% Ego, to Zero % Ego and 100% Love. This is the real task. Then what are you meditating on? A mind–defined silence. Actually, enjoying the feeling of the flow of Love is meditation.

SC: But all of us do it (meditation). You did it also Mahaprabu.

Mahaprabu: Yes, without knowing what Meditation was, I used to sit. I told you this.

Those who are filled with Love can enjoy the silence, but the reverse is not necessarily true. The moment you feel silence, you may not feel Love. But the moment you feel Love you will feel silence, but not as a word. Instead of silence there will be Joy. And that Joy will give you a satisfaction. This satisfaction ends in silence. A state of no oscillation. There is no want in that state. You are at equilibrium.

Instead if you start looking for silence, you will neither reach Joy nor Love. In the name of silence, you are simply doing something. See what people are meditating for. It is all happening at the brain centre. The brain is a muscular organ created by God to supervise, monitor and coordinate the functions of the body and protect it. For this purpose, thinking power was given. There is no problem with the thinking process, which is an ability of the brain. But a record in that brain that says 'I am a separate person' is the problem. The data is bad. Not the organ. So, trying hard to stop thinking is what many are chasing. You will go mad. There is a big difference between trying to stop thinking versus thinking stopping by itself.

The bad data in the brain centre is the problem. The whole system is now running with this bad data as the centre. Instead, the whole system should run based on Love as the centre. This bad data has to be invalidated, and it has to be done by you, since you are the one who recorded it. The Guru cannot do it for you. Once you remove this bad record, the natural spring of Love will come out. It wants to come out. The Master will show you the way to bring the love out. Just follow his words exactly. If you go deep inside Love you will find the pearl of self-knowledge deep within. It is not separate from Love. It is like the fragrance of the flower. You cannot separate the fragrance from the flower. So, the knowledge you are looking for is not here in the brain. It is buried in love. If you go with Love, you will attain it.

October 13th, 2022
Early AM, Sitthalapakkam House.

Turiyam

Sri Mahaprabu was in deep Samadhi for some time now. It was around 2 AM. Then, after a prolonged silence he spoke, perhaps trying to articulate the state he was in. Turiyam. What is it? How is it different from the 3 known states. Which is the real one and how to abide in it. His mellowed voice, the silent aura of the pre-dawn hour, all contributed to the depth of the content that was pouring out of him. Nature showered its love too, at the end, as you will read.

Sleep, Dream, Waking, Turiya

Sleep actually does not exist. There is no such thing called sleep. It is an idea that has been recorded in the brain. The body needs rest. The organs, muscles etc are working a lot. They need a period of rest in order to rejuvenate themselves. It is a very natural process. And the body knows how to do it by itself, and when to do it. Mahaprabu realized this one day at a very very deep level and said 'Sleep does not exist.' That's why they call it 'sleepless sleep'. There is a sleepless state inside, yet there is sleep outside (for the body). This sleepless sleep state is Turiyam. *Thannaiyum maravamalum piridhondrai ariyamalum* – Not forgetting oneself and not knowing any other is called Turiyam. They call it the 4th state but actually it is the only state. For understanding it is kept as the 4th state. Waking, Dream, and Sleep being the 3 states and Turiyam being different from these three, it has been called the 4th state.

Actually there is only Tuiryam. Turiyam means *Vizhippudan kudiya oru iruppu* – Knowing about its own presence. A drop of this Turiyam, a ray of it reflecting in the brain has created these so-called ideas of waking, dream and sleep and these seem to be real. *It is like a ray of the sun reflects on something and started acting as the sun!* A ray of Turiyam, a ray of this Vizhippu comes out. That's why in the waking state we feel this Vizhippu (we know we exist, a knowing about our existence). In dream also there is this knowing. We know what happens in the dream. But it is not as clear as what happens in the waking state. The reflection is dull. More dull than this happens in sleep. But there is that ray. Otherwise how does one say 'I slept really well'. Did you ask someone to confirm this? How can you say it without knowing? Even in that very dull state, there is a ray of a knowing presence, because of which, the fact that I slept well was recorded.

This ray of Thuriyam called Vizhippu (knowing presence) is your chance to retrace the way back. Sleep is very dull. Dream is a little brighter than sleep. Waking is brighter than that. Turiyam is the brightest, the original form of these states. Therefore it is not a state 'other' than these 3. People even have given it an order, actually in reverse! Waking first, then Dream, then Deep Sleep then Turiyam. That is wrong.

SC: Yes, there is a notion that deep sleep is very close to Turiyam.

Mahaprabu: Actually, it is a dull form of it. This is just for your understanding. I'll give you an example.

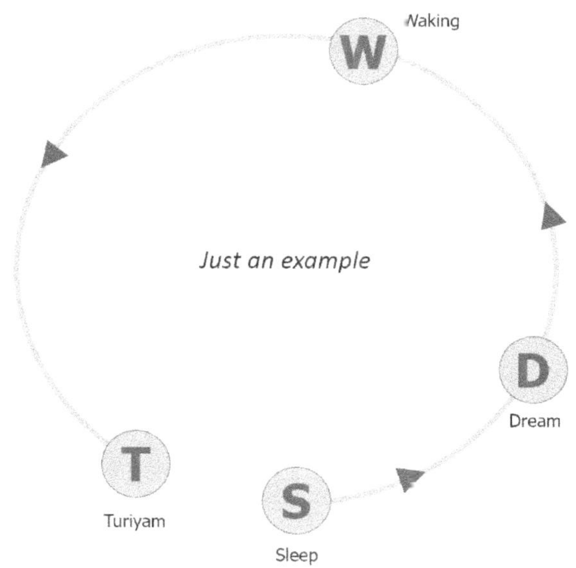

Take a circle with 4 points. Sleep, then further away is Dream, still further is Waking, and farthest from Sleep is Turiyam. But since sleep appears close to Turiyam on the circle, there is this misconception that it is proximal to that state. But to travel the circle is only one-way! (Laughing). If you look from dull to bright, then Sleep is the first, and Turiyam being the brightest is the farthest from sleep.

That is why Vaiai Subramaniam, a great Jnani and author of Yellam Ondre, says this beautifully about Turiyam: In *Odukkam* – the aspect of contraction or reduction, it appears to be much deeper than deep sleep. In *Vizhippu* –

knowing its presence, it is more aware than even the waking state. A very great book this is. It is the book that Bhagavan read and recommended. It is a pocket-sized book with the most precise and concise description of that Brahmam. See how that Brahma Sakthi, taking the form of Vaiai Subramaniam has spelled all this out, that too in Tamil. Now, look at his definition with my circle example. In contraction (*Odukkam*) it appears more deeper than sleep: the point of sleep is close to Turiyam. And in knowing its presence, (*Vizhippu*) it is much stronger than the Waking state. He even says, "Actually there is only this one state called Turiyam at all times. Waking, Dream and Sleep are like one long dream."

See, he calls sleep a dream. It does not exist in reality. Now look at it from this point of view. Start with Dream on the circle. Waking is a stronger Dream, because at least in Dream you say that it was a dream. But Waking you believe to be real. That is how strong it is. That is why Bhagavan says, 'Is there a world other than the mind?' So the Waking state is nothing but a brighter Dream. When seen from this standpoint, Sleep is the sharpest, since Waking is the dullest (you don't even know you are dreaming). So in one sense, you can say Sleep is the dullest, but from another point of view, Sleep is the sharpest of the three. Do you know what sleep is?

SC: An absence.

Mahaprabu: Yes, the absence of personhood, the individual, the ego. There is no Satchit. Turiyam is ever-present. It cannot be destroyed. You may not feel the presence of Turiyam. You are absent to the presence of Turiyam. 'You' refers to Personhood. So if sleep is the absence of personhood, then who has defined sleep? The Person! So how can it be real? And that same ego has defined Waking as the normal state. Actually, it is a very deep Dream! See how the mind tricks us. We believe Waking to be the real state.

SC: Yes, it is fully sustained by Personhood and therefore the most dangerous state! Full Nabarthanmai (personhood) but we have defined it as the normal state.

Mahaprabu: Yes, Waking is a terrible dream. A very strong dream. That's why Bhagavan says 'You think you are awake, but in my point of view you are sleeping.' Therefore, Sleep does not exist. But 'you' (personhood) define it as a state because you (personhood) have disappeared. You are defining this absence of an idea about yourself, and you are calling it Sleep. It is that point where the last idea about you is there. At all other times, you have strong ideas about you. When that idea drops, you call it Sleep.

Turiyam alone IS

Does the body care whether you drop the idea of a person or not? Does the body care whether you dream or not? Irrespective of all this the body exists. It appears, functions and disappears. The existence of the body is sensed by Turiyam. Turiyam alone exists. That knowing presence knows that Personhood rises in waking, Personhood dulls in a dream and Personhood disappears in Sleep. It is as though these 3 events arise out of Turiyam and contract back into it. [Mahaprabu acted out with his hands, something coming out of a single point, expanding and going back into the same point]

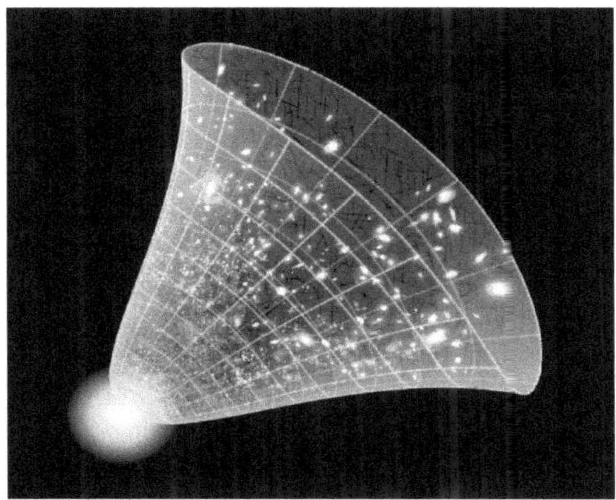

The above image is just an attempt at depicting what Sri Mahaprabu was trying to enact with the motion of his hands. Something expanding out of a single point and contracting back into itself. Please do not give this diagram any more importance than that.

So, what is it that comes out and goes back in? The starting point is Turiyam and the ending point is Turiyam. The same Turiyam alone exists. *It is like having a Torch with 3 brightness level switches. First switch dull light, Second switch a bit brighter. Third Switch much brighter.* The first switch can be compared to Sleep. The second to Dream and the third switch to Waking. In all states it is light. That light is Turiyam. You can understand it in the reverse too. Total light. Reduce the brightness with a switch and you call it Waking. Reduce further and it is a Dream. Reduce further and it is Sleep. Totally reduced it contracts into Turiyam. The whole universe is functioning like this (again using his hands to depict how from a single point it expands to the 3 levels and contracts back to that point). The whole universe is this Turiyam, and the various bodies are each like that Torch.

But the function in each Torch is the exact same. Expansion and Contraction. It is a cyclical process.

We are all stuck in the idea of those 3 levels. So, when one torch that is in the bright state sees another torch in the dullest state we say 'He is sleeping still!' 'I woke up' etc. We are defining things based on these so-called 3 states only. But a Jnani has realized that these 3 are just variations of the same light. And that all that exists is light alone. Turiyam is the only state. It alone appears as this. Again, this is just for your understanding. Nothing can describe it exactly.

Darkness and Brightness are nothing but levels of light. From a point, it itself comes out and goes back into itself. When it comes out, we say brightness. When it shrinks, we say darkness. It is like from a highly concentrated singular point something bursts out into a sphere of colourful crystals and contracts all the way back into that single point. These crystals are dogs, cats, humans, mountains, oceans, etc.

SC: When does that contraction happen?

Mahaprabu: I am talking about *Avyaktam* (unmanifest state). In the beginning, all these were unmanifest in that point. Today they are manifest. Again they will become unmanifest. The whole universe will. So anything and everything that comes out of this point has what? A strong connection to the Centre. That is why it is able to retrace its way back to it. At the macro level, at the Universe level, this expansion and contraction happens. At the micro level the same thing happens. I am talking about Turiyam, Sleep, Dream, Waking as seen by an individual. Turiyam expands from that point and returns to itself. I am seeing this exact same rhythm in the Universe. The harmony is the exact same. This appears short-term, but the universe appears long-term. And when these two rhythms coincide, you realize that the universe itself does not exist. This is the point of Realization. In that state, Turiyam is the point and Turiyam is the sphere and Turiyam is every single glitter in that sphere. The point is the sphere and the glitter. For example, the Arunachala hill that you see is nothing but a single glitter, no different from any other glitter. It is your brain that is defining these things are separate. For example, Tiruvannamalai is a creation in your mind based on the information brought in by your senses. Based on the sensory information you have defined 'This is a place, that is a mountain' etc. You have forgotten that you and that are the same. This separation has become a habit. Nothing is apart from Turiyam. That is why you like to go to natural and scenic places. Because there is a Unity there. You don't separate the mountains for example.

So, in reality something else exists. But we are living based on our own definition of things! *When you ARE the water can you distinguish a big wave or short wave or even a wave? A strong magnetic field is contained in a point. It expands to a large circle. It shrinks back. It is the same magnetic field at all times.*

All this cannot be understood by the mind. There is only one opportunity here for you: You can be the point or you can be the sphere. You cannot avoid the point. It is happening. The only thing you can do is to Realize and Dissolve into it. Once you have dissolved will you sit here talking about all this? *It is like a red glitter seeing a green glitter and saying that you are Red and I am Green, without knowing they have a common origin.*

This not-knowing and knowing is the whole game. Ignorance and Awareness. Between these two poles the whole play is happening. Whether the glitters are aware or unaware in ignorance, the rhythm of contraction and expansion will not change. So, all these definitions such as humans, living things, and non-living things are all false. That's why the Ribhu Gita strongly says 'Throw away this Bedha buddhi' Throw away this 'idea' of differences. It is only in your mind.

Even now just because you understand all this you are not in the *Abhedham* state (non-differentiating). Only when you experience the *Abhedham* state you will be in it. Otherwise you won't go there. But this understanding is essential for you to go to that *Abhedham* state. Otherwise you won't even make an attempt.

What to do?

So only one thing needs to be done. Consciously you should not allow the misconception. It must be done with total dedication. Having known all this, you cannot cheat yourself unconsciously. Any cheating will become aware to you. Since you are conscious to the understanding. It will tear you apart. It won't let you be in peace. So quickly come over to this side. This transit stage should be crossed quickly. Otherwise you will torture yourself. For Mahaprabu the sadhana period was 10 years: 1993 to 2003. In 1993 I had this understanding very clearly. So whenever I cheated myself, I was doing it consciously. It was torture. It was like each time I cheated it was as though I was cutting myself with a blade each time. From 1993 – 1997 it was terrible. I needed support. No one to help me. Any moment death can happen. Only in 1997 I made a strong decision that I cannot befool myself consciously. That I should cross this phase and come out of it. So 1997-2002, those 6 years I had taken the step consciously not to cheat. Now there was no guilt when I missed. Whatever suffering I encountered, I was willing to face. But I would not face the suffering that came from cheating. That self-suffering, conscious suffering I would not allow. I wanted freedom from that self-suffering. From 1993-1997 it was as though I had not even started the journey. But from 1997-2003 it was like someone had given me a map and knowingly or unknowingly I was progressing. But imagine the situation before that, when you know you have to go a place (meaning you have the understanding about suffering and you know what to do), the map also is given, but you are not even starting the journey.

Guru's help

So, give top priority to this and come out of the suffering. There is a natural rhythm happening continuously. (Again pointing to the contraction-expansion motion) You are able to accept it, correct? If so, then the Master's goal is to bring you into that rhythm. To do that, it creates a rhythm in the Master-Disciple relationship which matches the overall rhythm. Once you match this rhythm that the Master is creating for you, you will be in the track. You will understand then. The greatest help a Master does to a disciple is to bring him to this rhythmic state. Once that happens, you will understand.

See yesterday the content was all about Love. Today it spoke very deeply about Turiyam. All these are needed for you. These are entering your consciousness so that you are forced to complete this journey. You cannot cheat yourself anymore.

SC Notes:

When I first saw the clock after several hours, I realized it was 3:45 AM. Mahaprabu said it was time to leave. Coming outside with Mahaprabu, the lane was quiet. Several stray cows and dogs were sitting right in the middle of the street. Sri Mahaprabu spontaneously found a spot at the side and sat down on the road amidst them. He opened his bag and fed the remaining buns to the dogs. A hungry calf came by and shared the bun! Another calf joined. Then he fed them some grapes, which the starving calves devoured. The most touching thing happened then. One of the calves kissed Sri Mahaprabu on the cheek. By grace, these precious moments were recorded.

After Satsang, around 4 AM we came out on the street, heading towards the car. As always, there were dogs and cows resting there. This time, Sri Mahaprabu spontaneously sat down with them, and began to feed them.

Feeding Grapes

A kiss of gratitude from a calf

October 14th, 2022
Around 2 AM, Sitthalapakkam House.

Feeding the Brain

A very practical guide for how the words we use in daily life must change. Otherwise, we are only strengthening the wrong idea that has already been fed to the brain. Sri Mahaprabu speaks only this way and urges us to do so at all times, no matter who we are talking to.

The right usage of words

Sri Mahaprabu never encourages the use of words such as "Did you eat? I ate. Did you sleep?" etc. Instead, he urges us to say "Given food to the body? Given the body rest?" Even simple phrases such as "I came, I went" are replaced with "This came, This went" (referring to the body). Sri Mahaprabu speaks only this way with us. And not only with us. This (not I) has seen him speak like that with everyone. At work, at home, outside. No difference. Just recently it overheard Mahaprabu asking the head of the village, "Have you given afternoon food to the body?" He is a living example for us.

Mahaprabu: Don't say 'I ate'. Since it is the body that consumes food. Not the imaginary person. It is the body that moves. Likewise, saying 'I slept' is entirely wrong. The body needs 'rest and it knows when to rest. 'Gave rest to the body' is more appropriate. Words are important. Because, here we are trying to realize our True nature as a nameless formless being other than the body, but the language we use denotes the opposite, where we take ourselves to be the body!

Start applying these. Don't worry about others. They will think differently. But don't worry. This is called 'Living with the Fact', not with Philosophy, as Osho says. What we are talking about is fact. We are not imagining. We aren't speaking something that is not relevant to the Truth. No. The body is taking rest. Food was given to the body. 'I am' is the false one. So avoid saying 'I am sleeping', 'I ate' etc. You Are. Yes, no doubt. But not as I. Replace 'I' with 'This', but do it consciously. Make that separation clearly.

Clarity is needed

As we want to experience the Truth, we have to use words that can take us toward Truth and avoid all other words. Otherwise, we are giving the wrong information to the brain. As we feed wrong information, the brain will process it and produce the wrong result naturally. Using wrong data, we cannot expect the right result. Everything goes wrong.

We need not worry about other people. No need. It comes to our knowledge that the body needs to grow healthily, so food and comforts are needed, money needs to be earned, etc. All this has to be done, no doubt. We can accept the body. We can accept the world. We have to! We cannot say that the body and world are imaginations. They are there. The body is able to feel the heat from the sun. We are not imagining that there is heat. So, we should see things as they are. Likewise, we can do whatever is needed for the body. But clarity in the brain is very much needed. Giving the right information is essential. That you are an individual, that you are this body, is wrong information. The body, and feelings in the body, all are real. But 'i' is unreal. Focusing on that 'i', holding onto that 'i', living for that, and working to make 'me' happy is the worst thing we do. How can you work for an unreal thing? How can you ever make an unreal thing happy? You cannot.

So first we have to come out of this idea. Clarity should be given to the brain. You have given the data to the brain that I am 'xyz' and I have to do all these things, these are mine, etc. Totally wrong, finished! See, the body is given to us. And actually, you are not using the body. The one who has created the body is using it. It has all the rights to use it. It will use the body with or without your approval. Everything is perfect. Clarity in the brain is needed. Nothing else. Not even enlightenment. We should be very clear about that term enlightenment. How can you add light to that which is already bright? As you are light you are looking at me. The problem is because the wrong data which we have loaded into the brain, interferes continuously. And it is not the mistake of the brain. It is a servant. We are the boss. So be the Boss. (Please read the talk 'The Boss and the Servant' in this volume).

Being beyond body and world

So based on the wrong data, some wrong processing happens, and this is what interferes. The original Being is there, here and now. It does not doubt its existence. To confirm whether you exist or not, you need not seek any help. How are you able to say that you are here and now? Which is telling you? On what basis are you recognizing that you are here and now? What is that in the background which makes you feel that you are here and now? IT is here and now. The one which knows about its own existence is existing here and now. As it is existing, the body exists. I can see this existence as you. A formless one creates and exhibits forms. It has created the body. As it needs eyes, it has created eyes. And it has created vision. Sometimes it even creates defects! Loss of vision for example. But there is no doubt in its existence even when vision is lost, hearing is lost, touch is lost, or smell is lost. You won't see or hear or feel but you will be able to feel that you are here and now. That cannot be eliminated.

Mainly using the eyes and ears, you have wrongly recorded in your brain that 'This is me' (referring to the body). This has happened without any enquiry by the brain. It has the ability to analyze but cannot function on its own. As this is about knowing one's own existence, and as it exists beyond the brain, we cannot go there using the brain. IT can use the brain. But using the brain we cannot go there. We can understand up to a point but using the brain we cannot experience IT. When you ARE in that state, that experience can be recorded in the brain. But even that record is NOT the experience! It is like this: *With love I can embrace you. That can be recorded in a video. But in the video, there is no love! Love cannot be recorded.* Same thing here. The brain can record. But you cannot have the experience in the brain.

Therefore, asking so many questions after questions to know the one which cannot be reached by questions and answers, is futile. You can ask anything about the body or world. You can find answers and give understanding to the brain about everything else. But not this one. But due to the old habit of using the brain to understand things, we are trying to understand Existence, which is impossible. The last use of the brain is to understand that it is impossible to understand IT by the brain. Once the brain reaches this point, then the function of the brain will stop with respect to knowing the Being. We can use it for all other purposes but not here. People don't use their brains in all other things, but here they use it really well! What to do!

There is no problem with the world and body. It is not ours. Existence, Nature wants to come with a body so it comes. When it decides it is not needed it will drop it. It is HIS decision. IT wants to see ITs creations through the body so it created eyes. IT wants. Who are you? As IT wants to reproduce more and more and more to continue life in the world, IT has produced sexual organs so well. They match perfectly in all species. IT wants to enjoy; IT wants to live. But look at the amount of politics created by the human mind on the topic of sex. You have not created or decided on the organs. In your body, each and every organ is so important for Existence. But in our brain we have recorded the sexual organs alone with guilt. *People don't even itch there freely!! They look around nervously. But itching their face or hand, they do it perfectly, naturally.* See the pollution in the brain. Just for example, I'm pointing out. Sex is the basic component of human politics. Like this, we can talk about all kinds of feelings.

Existence is not a Subject or Matter. It is a powerful being, full of Love, Energy, and Wisdom. It can exist with form and can exist without form. Whether it is with form or without form, for Existence there is no difference. It is like this: *You may wear clothes or not wear clothes. It makes no difference to the organs in the body. Externally it will look different but there is no change in your body or its functioning.* The same thing with Existence. It may be with form or without form. No difference for That. So, whether IT is with a body or not, Wisdom is there, Intelligence is there and Love is there.

A wonderful synonym for Existence is Godliness. Because we have already given enough definitions for God and Godliness, therefore the brain can easily accept it. We know human is limited; God is unlimited. We ARE nothing but Godliness. We are droplets of pure Godliness. We should feel very proud about that.

Relationship with Body

Atma is beyond the body. Its existence does not depend on the body. So is it right to say 'I am in this body?' So far, we have been using it in that sense, but even that is wrong. (This talk was directed towards a disciple. Mahaprabu pointed out that the disciple now had the maturity to understand and accept what he was about to say). You are NOT IN this body. The body is in YOU. You are always an unlimited one. How can an unlimited one limit itself inside the body? That is also wrong data given to the brain. 'I am in this body'. NO. The body is in YOU. It has reached You. You can exist without the body. You are going to exist without the body. You don't need the body. The body needs you. You are the All-Pervasive one. You are thinking it is inside you, but NO. You are All-Pervasive. A body can be attached. And at a particular point be detached. At the early stages of understanding, we typically say 'You are in the Body' but as the understanding matures, we should realize that it is not true. So do not imagine you have entered a body and are locked. Even now you are a limitless being. How can you then limit yourself be limited within this body? If you accept that, then you are accepting that You are limited. No. The Body is limited. It has its starting and end. The body is with You, and You can be without it.

About Death

Think about these things and let your brain be engaged with all these things. Instead, you have directed your brain to go in the wrong direction. It is a poor servant, obeying you. So, give it the right data. Then your brain will assimilate it. It will search. You will meditate. Once you have the bodiless experience you will realize that you are not in the body, the body is in you. And if that is the case, why worry so much about the body? Yes, take care of it, but don't care!

Since the body is attached to us, it is a burden. When this burden is removed from us, how will we feel? We will feel happy. When some disease comes and leaves the body, we feel fresh! Similarly, when the body leaves at death, we will feel free. We will celebrate death. Only when you can celebrate death can you celebrate everything. Only those who can celebrate death can celebrate life. Those who fear death are afraid to live. So, to Live, we have to understand clearly who we are and what death is.

Real education

This should be the lesson in schools and colleges. Education to earn money should be the last. The first lesson should be spiritual health. The second should be mental health. The third lesson should be about physical health and the last lesson should be about Vitamin M − Money! But it is all upside down. The first lesson is about earning, and there is no lesson about Spirituality. That's why everything is upside down. See how education is influencing life. As spiritual seekers of Truth it is our responsibility to pave the path for the next generation so they can travel with the right education. Without doing this service you cannot expect great things in your life. God will not give. I know. God will take every drop of you in the process of revealing himself. Every drop of your blood must be given in service to Him. That is why even though this state is possible for all humans, very, very few are attaining this state. Whatever path you take, Jnana, Bhakti, give it your all. When will you give it totally? When you don't own it! When you don't own the body, me or mine. Annamalai Swami gave himself totally to Bhagavan. He attained that state.

So, stop thinking you are a human. It is wrong data that you are feeding the brain. With tremendous courage remove it. Don't bother about others. We are moving from madness to Godliness. When we move towards Godliness, we can see the Godliness in others despite their madness. That is the solution. Instead, we are seeing each other from our mad point of view. This only leads to problems. So let us move towards this great destination. From our destiny to the destination.

Let us sincerely thank the Supreme Power and pray to that Power to keep all our brains always in the right path and may our brains always long for the love of the Supreme Power.

Very happy to have all of you in Satsang.

October 29th, 2022
Rest House at Paliapattu

Sleep, Waking, Sat Cit Anandam

Why a seeker must overcome sleep. What happens during sleep? How does the ego rise on Waking? What is behind it? And how does one go about dissolving the ego. These questions have been tackled at a depth that we had never heard or read before.

While chanting verse 23 of Ulladu Narpadu, Sri Mahaprabu stopped to say a few things about Sleep. A disciple asked some questions about this topic. A very in-depth explanation came forth from Sri Mahaprabu. None of us had ever read about or heard from such depth before.

This is the verse 23 and its meaning:

Naan endru iddheham naviladhu
Urakkathu naan indru endru yaarum ravilvadhillai
Naan ondru yezundhapin ellam yezhun
Indha naan engu yezhum endru
Nunmadiyaal yen

This body does not say 'I'
No one says I did not exist in Sleep
Once the 'I' rises, everything arises
Enquire where this 'I' rises
With a very keen intellect.

Mahaprabu: The 3rd line: When the 'I' rises, everything rises with it. Yes, when 'I' rises, family, duties, tasks, work, aspirations, society, rules and all kinds of garbage arise. Then Bhagavan says "Keenly observe where this 'I' arises from." In the previous line, Bhagavan says 'We don't say I did not exist in deep sleep.'

Sleep must be overcome

We have to go past sleep.

At some point, everyone must necessarily cross this point called sleep. The word sleep conveys an absence. But the fact that you say you slept well means that you were there. Which means that you did not sleep. Yes, you were not aware of the world or your body, or your name or gender, etc, but in the morning you know without a doubt that you slept very well. How did you know? This is where the enquiry needs to be done. You have been a witness, but you don't know this. You don't know anything about that witness.

But right now, in the waking state, you have no doubt who you are: A disciple, a Son, a Male, a Father, etc. But when it comes to sleep, there are two things we know: There was an experience of very peaceful sleep. There was something that witnessed and enjoyed that experience. There, who were you? Were you a male? A Son? A disciple? You don't know. That's the mystery.

The only way to know who you were then, is to cross, sleep. Overcome sleep. As long as you succumb to sleep you will never know. That is why if you notice, our Satsangs go past 2, 3, or 4 Am. Sometimes they start only at midnight. We need to win over sleep. Without crossing it you will never discover who you were in that very subtle state. You were there but there is a darkness about your presence. It has to be keenly observed. But as you get into the sleep zone, you get lost in sleep. How can you discover it then?

In the waking state, you are active, fresh, energetic and you want to exhaust that energy. So, what do you do? You go out, work, do this and that, buy that, visit some place. Finished. It won't let you stay quiet. In such a state you sit for Dhyanam (meditation). What will be the quality? So much energy is available to go outward. How can you do Dhyanam? *It is like trying to stop an accelerating train in its tracks with your two hands in front.* How can you meditate? All your senses are ready to go out due to the energy. Yet you sit. Then you feel that you are unable to control your thoughts. But when you are with the Master, he knows which is the right time to meditate. Just like a mother knows what is the right time to feed the baby. A real Master knows when is the right time to meditate.

No matter what, you have to cross the sleeping zone. Without conquering sleep, you cannot attain Jnana. Jnana belongs to Awareness. Sleep is the opposite of Awareness. The two cannot coexist. Beyond sleep, deep inside there is a You. This is what Bhagavan points out: *Urakkathil naan indru endru yarum navilvadhillai.* – No one says I did not exist in deep sleep

D: While sleeping, the mind subsides. All identities are lost. On waking, it is the mind that says I slept well, correct? Or is it Atma that says it?

Mahaprabu: It is the mind that says I slept. Without knowing that it subsided, it says 'I slept well'. Yet it senses that there was a deep peace.

D: So, when does the mind totally disappear?

Mahaprabu: This sleep, which is by the mind, is one with ignorance. In sleep, the Gavanam, Attention subsides. It is not totally gone. That is why the mind says 'I slept well'. But there is a state where a kind of sleep is possible where the mind is totally off i.e., the mind does not just subside as in sleep. It is called Vizippu Unarvu or Turiyam.

Sri Vaiai Subramaniam in his epic book Ellam Ondre says this about Turiyam:

Vizippil nenaivai kaattinum adhiga vizhippulladhayum;
Odukkathil Thookatthai kaatilum adhigam odukkam ulladhayum irrukkum.

Turiyam is more wakeful than the waking state and more withdrawn than deep sleep.

This *odukkam*, this subsiding or withdrawal is called Sleepless Sleep. So in sleep, it is incorrect to say there is no mind. There is a deposit of ego there. Just that it does not have all the ideas that it has during waking, but it is still there. For example, *if 10 boys called Ram are sleeping in a room, when one of the Ram's mother comes to the room and calls out the name Ram, only the Ram who is her son will wake up. And if he doesn't, another Ram will hear it, and wake up the son named Ram.* This shows that a trace of the ego is still there. Yet in sleep, there is an experience of deep peace since the sukshma shariram (subtle body) went very close to Atma, but it is still one of ego. It is one of darkness, since on waking you are unaware of the actual experience that you had.

The Gavana shakthi, the ability of Attention, is something that comes from Atma. In verse #22 Bhagavan says

Madhikku oli thandhu
Ammadhikkul olirum madhiyinai
Ulle madakki
Padhiyil padhitthidudal andri
Padhiyai madhiyal madhitthidudal
Enngan madhi

The Divine gives light to the mind and shines within it. Except by turning the mind inward and fixing it in the Divine, there is no other way to know Him through the mind.

Padhi lendhu dhan madhi veliyila vandhadhu - From Atma alone comes the Ability of Attention. *Padhi* means Atma. *Madhi* means Ability of Attention. In sleep, the fact that you slept well, comes in front of that Attention. Because Attention is an aspect of Atma. It is Self-Aware. On waking, the first thing that comes to this Attention is the Peace, Joy that was experienced in sleep. Since Peace, Joy is also an aspect of Atma. That is to say that one aspect of Atma called Attention, experiences another aspect of Atma called Joy, Peace. To put it in other words, Sat Cit Anandam is Atma. In this, Cit is that aspect of Atma called Gavanam, Attention. That Joy is the aspect of Atma called Anandam. In that deep sleep, Cit and Anandam are felt. But what is missing? Sat. The state of Jnana is when all three are felt as one. In sleep, only a partial experience is felt. It is not a total experience.

On Waking, the Cit which had Anandam in its view during sleep, now loses that Anandam. Bhagavan says (verse 23 above), *Naan ondru ezhundha pin ellam yezhum.* When the I rises, everything rises. On waking, what is coming out as I? It is the Cit. That is why they say this whole world is the play of Cit. Cit dominates. So if you really want to experience the Joy, the Anandam of Atma, which has to subside? Cit has to subside. Only when the Cit subsides, Anandam will be felt.

So in this song, Bhagavan talks about the two extremes of Cit. One is Waking, where Cit dominates and everything arises. The other is in Deep Sleep where Cit is very subdued. In that subdued state, it feels the Anandam of Atma. So in both states there is Cit. But we should not confuse that Cit with the Ego, because Ego strengthens as you come out while waking. On waking, the Cit misses the peace of Atma, and starts looking for it outside, through the senses and mind. This Cit in a kind of impure state is called Ego. Ego comes after Cit. Who feels the Ego? It is Cit. When Cit is in pure form it is Cit. The same Cit in its impure form is called Ego. When the impurities go, it is the pure Cit, the aspect of Atma. (Further down Sri Mahaprabu describes the relationship between Cit and Ego in detail.)

How to make the Cit turn inward

In order for the Cit to turn inward, it needs to subside. So how do you subside Cit in the Waking state? You cannot. But what you can do is subside the Nabarthanmai, Ego. As you keep reducing and reducing the Ego, the Cit behind it will also subside. As the Cit subsides and subsides, the Anandam, peace, joy increases. The more one stays in that state of Anandam, the more one abides and stays there, the Cit will eventually turn inward and realize the permanent source of that Joy, which is Sat. There Cit merges and the purna (full) state of Sat Cit Anandam alone remains.

Realize that there is only one thing here. It is of the nature Sat Cit Anandam. It is an indivisible unity. Just for explanation's sake, I am breaking it up into 3 aspects so you can understand. Even before you asked the question, you are Atma, while asking also you are Atma, and even now you are the same Atma. That same Sat Cit Ananda Swaroopam (The real nature). But even though I have explained all this and you have understood, only when you start to experience this for yourself, your questions will subside. Only when you have experienced it totally, does real life start.

How to reduce the Ego?

As Bhagavan says *Nun madhiyal yer*. Observe it with a keen mind. So Nun Madhi, a keen intellect is needed. Who has such a keen intellect? A very peaceful mind. An agitated mind cannot observe keenly. Jealousy, tit for tat, agitations all these durgunas (bad traits) are the blocks. A mind filled with peace, a sattvic mind, a pure nirgunam (no gunas) state is where nun madhi is possible. Otherwise your gunas will keep dragging you away. The struggle of the gunas reflects as struggles in the mind. In the nirgunam state the mind is like a perfect mirror. Then nun-madhi is possible. In front of such a keen Awareness, whatever appears will be keenly observed. With such a sharp intellect, when you look at where the "I" arises, where will it take you? **Using Cit you will reach Sat.**

What are we missing? The permanent one. It is Sat that we are missing. The permanent one is what we are missing. We (the Cit) know only about the impermanent. Everything we know is impermanent. That's why we feel so insecure, so afraid. And that is why we are trying to hold on to so many things to overcome this, but it does not work since they are all impermanent. But Cit itself is permanent. Imagine, from young a permanent thing Cit is seeing death all around it. Things end, people die, and our own bodies are also deteriorating. As it keeps on seeing impermanence and death, it loses its hold on life. It searches to see if there is anything in this world that is permanent. Actually, IT is the only permanent one, but it looks everywhere else. That is why Sadhu Om says "Having forgotten itself and taken the body to be itself, having looked all over for it, when will it finally abide in the heart?"

So Nun Madhiyal, with a sharp brain, see where the 'I' rises. As you keep on doing it, you will reach Sat. Cit will see that all there is, is permanence, permanent happiness. Then fear disappears. Living starts from there. Living with Anandam. This is truly living.

Thinking

People want to be without thoughts. That is not possible. As long as there is the body, in order for it to operate, thinking is essential. *When the hardware (body) dies, then there is no need for software (thinking). Until the hardware operates, the software is needed.* So one cannot be without thoughts. But people keep trying to be thoughtless. They make that state a target. Instead, the target should be living without Nabarthanmai (individuality or personhood or ego). Then in Dhyanam there is a possibility of a thoughtless state, that too temporarily. That state is when there is a possibility for Cit to reach Sat. In that state Cit, which is Gavanam has nothing in its focus. Because when there is no Nabarthanmai, Cit has nothing to do (nothing else comes to its attention). Then a peace, an Anandam is felt by Cit. The very same happiness that it felt in sleep is reflected or experienced in this thoughtless state too. Cit will recognize this. It finally has found what it has been missing all the time.

Two possibilities now

Now that Cit has found this peace and joy, two things are possible: The newfound experience of Anandam will become known to the ego. This is a dangerous point especially if you have not surrendered to a living Master. We shall see why. First, this gives a newfound energy. See, just waking up from sleep gives you fresh energy, using which the ego wants to go out into the world. It doesn't want to sit for meditation. Correct? That is for just the joy of sleep where you are not even aware during the experience of joy. Imagine the energy from having gone into a deep thoughtless state filled with joy! The ego will want to share it, celebrate it. Your attitude will be: I have found this wealth after having suffered, having practiced for so many years. This is great, this is enough! This is where seekers leave the path and start their own Satsang! They will share their experience, attract followers, start an organization, etc. But the seeker knows very well that he has not attained stability in that Experience. An incomplete journey. Yet he disregards it and goes outward. The newly formed patterns in the brain are quickly over-written by the ego through its outward activities. It is over. The seeker falls down the ladder into suffering again.

When the seeker is with a Master on the other hand, this risk is greatly reduced. If the seeker is in Surrender, the Guru will make sure the disciple continues on the path. The disciple will continue the attempts to stay inside and look to repeat this search and enjoy the feeling again and again. He will not leave the path at this stage. As he does it repeatedly, he becomes familiar with going into that state of joy and coming out. Going and coming out repeatedly. Then after a point, the Cit will look to go even beyond that. So far it has only been experiencing Anandam, but is not still established in Sat. Once it is established in Sat, then Cit will merge and Anandam will also merge. This is Samadhi. In Samadhi both anandam and arivu (Cit) will be in odukkam, totally subsided. It is almost like death. It is close to the origin – aadi. Hence the name Samadhi – Aadhikku samam, equal to the origin. To go there, Anandam and Cit should be subdued totally. In samadhi, the ego is totally gone. This is the state of Mukti, Liberation. Then there is no more birth.

But to get to this point of stability, if one is not careful, several births can be taken. That is why the Guru insists on Surrender till the very end. The seeker just has to follow the Guru's guidance and stay with him till the Guru says. This is how it was in the old days. Buddha was very strong in this. He would not even talk about the Joy of Atma He knew it would be a distraction for the disciples. Till the end, he tried to keep them in Surrender.

Relationship between Cit and Ego

[Follow up question and Sri Mahaprabu's response]

SC: What is the relationship between Cit and Nabarthanmai (Ego)?

Mahaprabu: Cit is like pure light. Ego is like a coloured glass. When Cit goes out through the coloured lens of Ego, a red lens for example, everything is seen as red. This red colour in the example refers to the strongly recorded thought in the brain that I am an individual; I am this body. It is a just a thought, a record in the brain. The light of Cit hits the brain and sees everything through this record. The whole thing is hinged on this 'I' thought. And it will forget so many other things but not this. Mainly because it is strongly identified with the body. The light of Cit on the body has created a record deep down in the brain associating the 'I' thought, with the body's appearance. This is Nabarthanmai, ego. It is very deep. This association is what Bhagavan calls Chit-Jada-Granthi. The knot that ties Cit to the Body. This is why in the old days, mirrors were not encouraged. Every time you strengthen this association with the body, this ego gets strengthened, and its effect on Cit becomes stronger and stronger. Because, it is Cit that engages with the Ego.

It is like this: *From the banana stem, a strand is removed and used as a thread to string flowers for garlands. In doing so repeatedly, the thread takes the smell of the flowers.* Here think of the flowers as Cit, and the thread as the Ego. Similarly, due to close association over many births, the Ego (thread) in association with the Cit (flowers) seems to take on the property of Cit and appears to have a separate existence of its own (smell of the flowers).

So, this is the answer to your question: What is the relationship between Cit and Nabarthanmai? It is the relationship between the thread and the flower. See, from the smell you can't even tell whether it is the thread or the flower. Due to the same smell, you are confused that the thread is the flower. That is why you are even asking this question: What is the difference between the thread and flower? They both smell the same!!! (Laughing). Your own confusion appears genuine to you! Actually, you are that Cit even while asking this question and should have no doubt!! But this example will clear it up.

Keep a distance between Cit and Ego

So, just like separating the thread from the flowers for a long time will eliminate the smell of the flower from the thread, being without the ego for a prolonged time will remove this confusion in Cit. *For instance, at this stage if your wife really calls you 'Hey, you dog' you will become upset soon or definitely at some point. Because the thread (ego) is very very close to you the Cit. But if my wife calls me 'Hey Mahaprabu, you dog' there won't be any impact. Because I have kept my thread – Ego very very far away. That too I have only kept the ego thread only for you, the disciples' sake. So that you can call me Mahaprabu and I can respond.*

We can and must keep a distance between the Nabarthanmai (Ego) and Cit. Only then you will even know which is which. Cit or Ego. It can be done and must be done. Keep on observing the Ego keenly, like Bhagavan says.

Futility of asking questions

Even though I explained this to you and you understand, it is still a borrowed one. You have to experience it for yourself. The Cit will not subside. It is used to going out. So it will keep asking more and more. You have to drop the Nabarthanmai (ego). But without dropping it you will be asking. This is a phase. Let the doubts come.

Cit always looks to know things. But your job is what? To drop the ego. instead of that, you will be asking questions. In that guise, the ego will continue.

See, you know exactly what ego is. You also know what Unarvu (feeling of existence) is. And you know that the two are different. And you know exactly what needs to be done? Drop Ego. Hold on to Unarvu.

SC: Right! Then why all these questions (Realizing the folly of asking).

Mahaprabu: Yes, this is how it will continue to exist. OK, next question, next question! Because it is used to this. Since the Cit is not able to touch the Unarvu, since it is not able to drop the ego, it keeps searching. It makes you ask. This needs to subside. Because there is no end to questions. When you get an answer to a question, from that answer another question will arise. From that answer, another question. This became a habit.

And for how long can you ask? As long as you don't Realize, you will keep on asking. But what is stopping the Realization? The Ego (which is asking)! (Laughing). This pattern needs to be understood carefully by you. See, no matter what, when will you get all the answers to your questions?

SC: When I experience it myself.

Mahaprabu: (Laughing). Yes, when you Experience it. So if you keep on asking, you are simply delaying what needs to be done. Because no matter what you get from the question, it is not important. Realizing, Experiencing is important. Not asking. So see which direction you should be heading.

This needs to be understood deeply by you. Understanding is maturity. In that maturity alone you will naturally stop asking. You will move steadily towards Experience. Also where are the answers to all your questions? Inside you. The only thing to do is to keep on moving towards Experience. Everything will be resolved only when you Experience the Truth yourself. I have shown you what needs to be Experienced. The Guru wants you to move towards it steadily.

These questions are not being asked by you intentionally or planned. They are coming. Till you deeply understand the uselessness of this, and the danger of it, you will continue to ask. You can ask. The Guru can tell. But the answer is not yours. It is a borrowed one and will not do you any good.

SC: It is like I keep asking you how a rose smells and you keep describing it, but until I smell it myself I will never know.

Mahaprabu: Definitely. So, questioning is a habit and we need to come out of it. Serving the Master is key. Buddha never allowed disciples to ask questions. It is said that for 2 years you had to stay quiet and just follow him. No questions. Even the one question as to why we are not allowed to ask questions, should not be asked. Beyond that, if the seeker asked questions, Buddha would keep mum. He wouldn't even turn his head. He was a great scientist, Buddha. That's why Osho says 'I like Gautama Buddha. The depth of consciousness that he has reached directly and perfectly, no other human has achieved.' Now, you might have a question about this too! (laughing). I understand the basis from which Osho has said this, but you don't know that. You are understanding that from your base. So, questions may arise in you. What Osho means is that Buddha was firmly entrenched in that height and never ever compromised. There is no difference in Jnana. Just that he never ever left that height. He never came out for anything or anyone. He stayed there.

November 6th, 2022
Rest House at Paliapattu

Surrender then Enquiry

A very important talk on how Self-enquiry should be done. Sri Mahaprabu goes into depth about the fundamental confusion, the difficulty and risks associated with practicing Self-enquiry in isolation, and as always, he guides us in the right way. The way that has a very high chance of success.

While chanting verse 27 of Ulladu Narpadu, Sri Mahaprabu stopped and said that we need to observe something very keenly. Here is the verse for reference.

Naan udhiyaadhu ulla nilai
Naam adhuvai ulla nilai
Naanudhikkum taanam adhai naadaamal
Naanudhiya thannizappai saarvadevan?
Saaraamal
Thaan adhuvaam thannilaayil nirpadevan?
Satru

When the 'I' has not arisen,
In that state We are That.
Without searching where the 'I' arises
How can one accomplish one's own extinction, from which the 'I' does not revive ever?
Without that attainment how is it possible to abide in one's true State, where one is THAT?

The Confusion

In this Atma Jnana sadhana (practice of realizing the Truth) there is a lot of confusion in the world. If we are not careful, we will continue to be identified with the body, this life and not come out of it. There is nothing wrong with identifying with the body or this life. But identifying with it and having forgotten that we have done so is the problem. For example: *Say you are someone, who really enjoys acting in plays. By profession, you are a farmer. But you love acting. In a play, yours is the role of a policeman. All dressed up, you act so well. Everyone appreciates your performance. Great. But after the play is over, if you get off the stage and believing that you are a policeman if you head to the police station and behave like you work there, what would happen? They will take you to the mental hospital.* Like that person, we as the Atma, as someone who celebrates life, can enjoy and love this world and all of creation. It would be the greatest celebration. That is fine. *Just like the actor enjoying his performance on the stage and giving happiness to others too.*

But the problem starts when we a) Totally forget our true identity and b) Also forget that we have identified with the body and world, and therefore c) Believe ourselves to be the body in this world. Instead of a nameless, formless, ever-happy being, we live believing that this body is me, these things are mine, I am separate from others, etc. In this way, we have made the world a madhouse. So, whenever you meet anyone don't forget the fact that 'I am a mad person and this person in front of me is also deluded.' Remembering as much as possible that I have succumbed to a madness and so has everyone around me, is the real solution for our madness.

We are droplets of Creation, appearing in this world to enjoy life, to celebrate life with everyone. Instead, we are trapped in what seems like hell. Do apples, oranges, lemons have any problems? Atma, the Supreme Power has created all these with the perfect nutrients for those who consume them. Where is the sadness in this? The first step in spiritual practice towards enlightenment is portrayed as - The world is miserable. We need to come out of this misery. Yes, when looked at from ignorance, the world is full of misery. And when the ignorant communicate this message to other ignorant people, it only strengthens that belief in all. The speaker and listener are all ignorant. But looked at with Wisdom, this world is Anandamayam - Full of Joy. And when you speak from Wisdom, and it is listened to with intelligence and discrimination, the fact will be clear. Because everyone has an ignorant portion and an intelligent portion in them. And when a man of Wisdom speaks, it is received by the intelligence portion of the listener, even if he is ignorant. When an ignorant man speaks, it is received by the ignorant portion of the listener only.

Therefore, be clear. Living in this world and enjoying its creations is not a problem. Having forgotten who we are, and imagining ourselves to be a limited person who is suffering is the problem.

Bhagavan in this verse, first says *Naan udhiyadhu ulla nila* - He uses 'I' here. The state where 'I' don't arise. But in the next line he says *Naam adhuvai ulla nilai* - Here he does not use 'I'. He says *Naam* - Us, We. He could have used 'I' for both. But he is so intelligent. Because only the 'I' is separate. When referring that That, he uses 'Us' implying unity.

Then he says

Naanudhikkum taanam adhai naadaamal
Naanudhiya thannizappai saarvadevan

Without observing where the 'I' rises, how can the ego disappear?

The practical difficulty with Enquiry

Reading the above lines, everyone sits down and closes their eyes. This is the next madness. Because if you sit and keep looking at the 'I' it will seem to disappear for some time. You feel good. Then you get up and look at someone. Instantly the 'I' comes back entirely. Till you sit the next time you will be totally operated by the 'I'. Then you sit and observe the 'I'. It might disappear. Again when you come out and act in the world the 'I' will totally run you. Again you sit. Again it comes back. When will this ever end? Very very difficult. Also, if you sit for an hour, only a very small percentage of that is actually when the 'I' disappears. The rest of the time is for all kinds of thoughts, recent happenings, future thoughts, and even thoughts about sadhana and Bhagavan. So really throughout the day if you add up the number of minutes in which the 'I' was absent, it is almost none. And the rest of the time (99% of your day) the 'I' is really strong. And you won't even know you are being operated by the 'I' at those times.

The point is, it is not possible for most ordinary people to continuously observe where the 'I' arises for more than a few minutes. Another risk is the 'I' itself is likely to divide into two, where one half pretends to watch the other half. You won't even know this is happening.

So the practical issues with this are: 1) For more than a few minutes you cannot sustain the observation of the place where the 'I' arises 2) Rest of the day the Ego has taken over and 3) Beyond these two if you try hard and force yourself to sit down with closed eyes, it still won't last. Why? Because the vasanas, likes-dislikes, karmas, are all a kind of energy in you that will push you outwards. They will not let you sit.

So the whole system is trying to push you out, but your memory will torture you saying 'I did not meditate; I did not observe the I; I did not meditate. I didn't observe the I.' Because you have loaded into your memory that you have to observe the place where the 'I' rises. But you are unable to. This pair of opposites: I should observe vs. I did not observe, will torture you. This is the practical difficulty.

Enquiry in a State of Surrender

Bhagavan knowing this, without saying it outwardly, has quietly guided the real disciples closely and tried to mature them by keeping them in surrender. He might have spoken a lot about self-enquiry but what he implemented as the path was Surrender. That is why he said "Everyone wants Moksha. But when I ask them to give themselves to me, they do not." What is this but Surrender? His path was surrender and self-enquiry the vehicle. Imagine a vehicle traveling without any path. How can it reach its destination? Therefore Surrender and Enquiry have to go hand in hand. Why? Because when you are in Surrender, your likes and dislikes will come out. But you will Surrender them to the Guru. 'Oh Gurudeva, I have done it without knowing. I surrender everything to you.' The Guru will guide you accordingly. Like this, every time your ego rises, you surrender it at the feet of the Guru. He makes sure you don't hold yourself responsible and encourages you to move forward in surrender. Over time, this surrendering habit takes over and weakens the out-going tendencies. He makes you reduce new likes and dislikes while making sure you don't brood over past regressions. Control shifts to the real you inside. A balance, a maturity grows. The energy to drag you out reduces. The ego weakens over time.

Side by side, he frequently exposes you to the ideas of knowing yourself, observing where the 'I' rises, the state where the 'I' has not risen, etc. As these understandings mature, and as Surrender continuously reduces the outward going energy, then when you do the enquiry, you will see the place where 'I' rises.

Because the very problem is what? You have strongly identified with this body and this life. You are one with it, tightly bound. In Surrender your whole attitude is, 'Gurudeva, this body and this life is not mine from this instant. This janma (birth) is for you alone. I am done. You are everything.' This is the only way you can separate yourself from the knot that has tightly bound you. Simply doing Enquiry will only shift your already strong identity towards an identity of a 'Seeker', or 'Bhagavan's devotee' or 'I practice Self-Enquiry'. Now it becomes very difficult for you to come out of this. At least when you knew about your ignorance there was a chance to free you. But once you believe yourself to have become a seeker of Jnana, a Ramana devotee, an Atma Jnana practitioner; once you believe you have got all the information from Bhagavan and other Jnanis, and that you know it all, then you actually start to believe that you are no longer ignorant. You might even start Satsang for others! Now how can you be freed? One who accepts his ignorance has a chance of being freed. But if you believe you are not ignorant, it is very, very difficult.

Never Separate the Two

Therefore, Atma Saranagathi (Surrender) and Atma Vicharam (Enquiry) should never be separated. Bhagavan did not separate the two. Although he could have emphasized Surrender strongly saying: Only when you stay in Surrender and then do Enquiry, you will attain Jnana. He did not emphasize it, but he never separated the two. Those who heard his message took the self-enquiry part alone and focused on it. They tried practising it, they spoke about it and wrote about it. All done using their minds. Our minds are good at separating things and taking what it needs. Surrender is conveniently ignored by the ego since it is really hard to give up one's ego to the Guru. Instead, enquiry was focused on. That is easy to take on for the mind. See, all their writings reflected it. Today when we read about Bhagavan, only self-enquiry is highlighted. They made self-enquiry its own path. Separate from anything else, especially Surrender.

[SC had paused transcribing as the call for Satsang came. Remarkably in that Satsang, Sri Mahaprabu read from a book of Bhagavan's talks where Bhagavan told a seeker, that if you want to attain Jnana, the only way is to Surrender to the Master and follow his instructions exactly. -Amazing]

Mahaprabu saw this clearly. He knows that Bhagavan knew the importance of Surrender as the basis upon which the relationship of Guru-Disciple exists. Without that platform, just self-enquiry will not result in Jnana. He knew that.

It is only when you stay in Surrender for a prolonged period of time, a) the old outgoing tendencies and old likes and dislikes will dissolve; b) the new egoistic tendencies will not rise; c) since there isn't much outgoing energy, the grip of the ego has weakened. Only then can you see clearly where the 'I' arises and experience the state without the 'I'.

So please don't separate the two. Only the one who is in Surrender can attain Jnana. This is the Truth. This is what Buddha taught and implemented. What I am telling you is very precious. It is coming from Experience. Only a sincere and serious seeker will know the value of this and implement it. Only he who knows the path and does the sadhana accordingly can attain Jnana. Without knowing the right path no matter what sadhana you do, even if you drink milk sitting in the lap of Bhagavan, or any Guru, nothing will happen. Surrender is the first requirement. This is what Osho said emphatically in one sentence: '*No Master can do anything unless the disciple surrenders himself totally, unconditionally*'. That is why Mahaprabu has had this printed and stuck on the wall behind him. Note that he didn't say just 'I cannot do anything'. He said 'No Master can do anything'.

The Only Way

Once you have truly, strongly decided that no matter what, I must realize the Truth, then this is the only way, the only path. And where will you get this strong resolve to realize the Truth? Only in Satsang with a real Master. Therefore, you should give the highest value to what? To Satsangam (association with a Jnani, as He is Sat). More than Jnanam, give value to Satsangam. That will take you to Jnana.

See what the great Jnani, Shankara said: *Satsangathve Nissangathvam, Nissangathve Nirmohathvam, Nirmohathve Nischalathathvam, Nischalathathve Jivanmukti.* – Being in Satsang leads to non-attachment, which in turn frees one from delusion. The result is an unoscillating state where the Reality can be experienced.

He gave us the formula for Jivan Mukti. It starts with Satsang. Who stays in Satsang? One who is in Surrender. The great Jnani and Advaitin Adi Shankara smeared vibhuthi all over his body and lived a life steeped in Bhakthi. He showed us how to live in Surrender to the Supreme Power.

Be in Surrender. Give your entire life. That is why Bhagavan wanted the disciple to give himself totally to him when he said 'Everyone wants Moksha but when I ask, they don't want to give themselves totally. Then how can Moksha be attained?'

Your attitude should be "God, Gurudeva, I am yours. My life is yours. It is in your hands. I have no say. No matter what happens. Just tell me what I have to do." Only then your outward energy, your likes and dislikes will reduce and reduce to the point of Nischalathathvam. In that unoscillating state when you do what Bhagavan says, "Keenly observe where the 'I' arises" only then you will see clearly what IS. But right now, you are in such an agitated state of mind, that even on the surface, things are not clear. Where will you get clarity deep inside?

See how one Jnani after another is coming to assist us. First Osho came, then Adi Shankara.

Jai Sri Satgurunath Maharaj ki Jai

Follow up

As usual, out of ignorance, later on SC asked Sri Mahaprabu: We are on verse 27 of Ulladu Narpadu. Why is it that in all these verses and in the remaining 13 verses there is not a single line from Bhagavan that Surrender is the first step? There is not even a mention of Surrender in Ulladu Narpadu.

Sri Mahaprabhu patiently answered this in great depth. In summary he said: In the Ulladu Narpadu anubandham (addendum), the very first verse by Bhagavan is this: *In the company of a sage, attachment vanishes; and when attachment is gone, illusion disappears. Freed from illusion, one attains stability, and thence liberation while yet alive. Seek therefore, the company of a sage.*

Verse 2: Not by listening to preachers, nor by study of books, not by meritorious deeds nor by any other means can one attain that Supreme State, which is attainable only through association with the sages and the clear quest of the Self.

Verse 3: When one has learned to love the company of sages, wherefore all these rules of discipline? When a pleasant, cool southern breeze is blowing, what need is there for a fan?

See, Bhagavan has actually said that Surrender to a Master is an unavoidable requirement.

[Again out of ignorance came the next question: Wondering why Bhagavan did Bhagavan bring up Surrender to the Master only in the Addendum? Why not at the very outset? For which Mahaprabu's gracious answer is summarized below.]

Bhagavan's devotees like Kavya Kanta Ganapati, Muruganar, etc were very reputed poets and scholars. They even had their own followers, right there in Ramanashram. If Bhagavan had put Surrender as the first step, do you think they would have accepted? No way. Imagine Bhagavan saying to each and every seeker: 'OK. First you surrender to me totally. Then we will talk about next steps.' What would have happened? Bhagavan knew this. He wanted the disciples to be in Satsang with him regularly. So he gave them material to think about. The direct path of Self-Enquiry! Now, the Ego is fine with that and will accept it. So everyone practised that. To practice it, they needed Bhagavan, so they stayed close to him. Same thing with Paramahamsa. He knew that Surrender to the Guru was the way and that the disciples had to be in Satsang with him. But this was Calcutta! Great intellectuals like Vivekananda, Rakhal, Gopal Chandra etc. So instead of Guru, he put God in front. He knew they wouldn't surrender to a God in a human form. He sang about the Mother in ecstasy. He made them sing about the Mother too! Seeing him, they all followed. Without knowing it, they all stayed in Satsang with him and slowly matured. At the outset if Paramahamsa or Bhagavan had said, 'First you must surrender to me', no one would have stayed! The goal of a Guru is to keep the disciple with him as much as possible.

[SC thinking to himself: I guess this is the answer to the question that has been with me for some time: Why is it that even though Mahaprabu reinforces Surrender as the first step, yet in his Padhayin Padigal (Steps towards Realizing one's true Nature) he put 'Surrender to the Guru' in Step #2, not Step 1. The first step is 'Dropping the habit of performing actions on the basis of the ego.' Step 1 is probably an entry point to Step 2 where the real transformation happens!]

Bhagavan had even said once: Do either one of these two. 1) Enquire who you are. Or. 2) Surrender to the Higher. Either way, he wanted the disciple to stay with him.

Only those who Surrendered, attained

So many were with Bhagavan. Almost none of them were in Surrender. They all followed the Enquiry path. We know the result of where they all ended. Now look at Annamalai Swami. He was not much educated. He knew two things. I want Mukthi. I want to be with Bhagavan. That's all. He soon surrendered totally to Bhagavan. And Bhagavan took care of him very closely, personally. Once when he saw him talking with other disciples, Bhagavan went to him and put his hand over the shoulder and said "Don't mix with them. Only scholarship is there." See how much care Bhagavan took. Once when Annamalai Swami decided to not do the construction work and left for Girivalam, when Bhagavan heard this, he stopped the Satsang midway and went to the construction site and did the work himself. See how tactfully he taught Annamalai Swami a lesson. He didn't ask him why he went nor did he admonish him. He showed him what was important, which was to do what the Guru says and to not yield to your likes and dislikes (going on Girivalam). Imagine what an impact it would have had on Annamalai Swami, seeing Bhagavan doing the work he was supposed to do! See, people were stunned. He stopped the satsang to do Annamalai Swami's work. That is how much he loved and cared for the disciple who was in Surrender. And after a few years, he once hugged and embraced Annamalai Swami with love, thereby giving him the experience. See, that experience cannot be given by words. He did it by touch. To whom? Only to Annamalai

Swami. Only to the disciple who truly surrendered. Why? Because Surrender is the only way. If you are not in Surrender, you are with your Ego. How can you get the ego-less experience?

Even when Annamalai Swami moved to Pelakothu, Bhagavan went and visited him and checked on him. He even took food for his disciple! So many lived in Pelakothu including Sadhu Om. There is no mention ever of Bhagavan visiting them at their homes. See how Surrender works! See the result! **Annamalai Swami attained Jnana.**

November 11th, 2022
Rest House at Paliapattu

Importance of Awareness

The Body and World are brought to our Awareness, which is an inbuilt ability in life. But we use it only to go outwards. Instead, we should use it to turn towards its Source. This is possible only in a human birth.

Awareness is everything. We all have awareness and we are aware. Otherwise, we won't be able to do all the things we do. But that awareness stops with outside things. It doesn't know itself. Like Osho says, the lamp illuminates things around it, but is dark right under it. Like that, with Awareness (Y) we see everything, but we don't enquire where it comes from and what is our relationship to that.

As something is existing here and now, the body is existing. How are we able to feel the existence of the body? Because of the one which is existing here and now (Call it Z). We may not know about that thing Z. But one thing is sure: Because of that Z which exists here and now, the Awareness Y is existing. The existence of the body and world are brought to the Awareness of THAT (Z) which is existing here and now, which we don't know of at this point. So, Awareness (Y) is the only key. With this Awareness we are able to see the world, and do so many things, but using the same Awareness we should know the origin of this Awareness, Z. That is missing here. Only using this Awareness Y, we can experience that Z which is here and now, from which that Awareness is produced. But no one is doing this.

Scientists and doctors know so much in minute detail about the body but are never aware of how they are aware of all this. They have so much information in their memory. Just because you have a great memory doesn't mean you have Awareness. You can store things in memory without being Aware. For example, a child memorizing something blindly, can recite it perfectly. But if you have Awareness, you will definitely have a good memory. Memory is tied to the brain. Awareness is tied to Life.

As you become more Aware of that Z, you are going closer to Uyir (Life). You will get close to Love. You will become more loving. But the brain still is there, with all its records. It will definitely interfere and pull you out. You will soon become the ego and judge the world around you. Also, you will take responsibility for things. See, you are not responsible for Awareness. But you will take responsibility for things brought to that Awareness. You might see something that appears as injustice and say 'I cannot take this anymore.' This is where Bhakti is so important. Actually speaking, you are not responsible for anything happening here. Truly realising that you are not responsible for anything here is Jnanam. You cannot even move your eyelid without His permission. See how people think they are responsible. A warden of a hostel, a father, a politician, a doctor... But as you get closer to the source of Awareness you will feel the love, and then the compassion. From that heart, when you sincerely ask, it will be given to you. Because you are close to the centre of Existence.

So, we cannot say our Awareness is complete. Because even though it knows so much about the body and world, it is totally unaware of the cause of Awareness (Z). Therefore our current awareness is incomplete. It doesn't know its own origin. Now we have to turn that Awareness towards finding its origin. 75% of our time must be spent on that. The remaining 25% should be spent on directing the awareness for the continuity of the body. Because the body is in that Awareness. In parallel we have to grow Bhakthi. Because you have so many ideas of ethics, right/wrong, good/bad in you. These will become an obstacle. But really all these are garbage. They are relative. What is good now is bad tomorrow. What is good to one is bad to another. They are all created by minds and are baseless. So many customs in society were good ones some time ago, but bad today. In North Korea, watching a Hollywood movie can get you in jail. Imagine the mindset of a person born there. His value system will be shaped very differently. So, what is needed in parallel is Bhakti towards God or Guru.

More than enquiring who am I, start with what you know. You know you exist. This is because, you are aware that you exist. In fact, it is the only thing you know directly. Everything else is learned, acquired and will all be taken away by death. Knowing this, will you run behind all this? Only a fool would. This is why Jnanis stay with their eyes closed. So they don't see the fools, and also with eyes closed, they feel THAT. So, give top priority to enquiring where that Awareness originates from. It has been with you for your entire life and for so many lives before. You have wasted all those moments.

The body is X. Behind that, is the Awareness Y. Using Y, X is seen and the world W is seen. This world W is common for all. i.e. the mountains, the oceans, the land etc. But depending on the body each has its own world. For eg. For a Fish, its world is all water. For a snake, its world is all ground and at a low altitude. For a human, the world is very different. Therefore, the world is in the mind alone. Our bodies (X) may be different. Each being's world (W) is different. But all beings have Awareness (Y). And behind that common Awareness (Y), there is also a common origin for that Awareness (Z). So, when you see things whether it is a dog or a snake or a human, see past the body (X) and go towards Y and then Z. These Y and Z are common for all. The quantity of Y differs from being to being. An ant may have 1 unit of Y, a human many more units, but the Quality of Y is the same in both. And Z is ONE and the SAME for ALL.

A human birth is extremely rare. It is only in this birth that we can turn towards our origin. Even though all beings have Y and Z as common, you cannot sit next to a snake and communicate with it about any of this. An amoeba has Y and Z too, but no sense abilities are developed. Only in the human birth can this be understood and taught. As it is so, we should use this birth as much as possible for finding out who we truly are.

———◆ ◄◄ ◆ ►► ◆———

December 10th, 2022
Rest House at Paliapattu

The 2 things you need to do

Being in Surrender and remembering the one which is existing here and now at all times, is the Sadhana. And you have to give yourself 100% for this. Only then it can happen.

The whole practice is to remember, and recollect the formless and nameless being which is existing here and now. By a constant, continuous effort of remembering, recollecting it, throughout the day, continuously, regularly, sincerely, one day a moment will come after which we need not remember, need not recollect.

Take the example of a little girl. Especially in Tamil Nadu. As a child, she would be free and play equally with boys. As she starts to grow a little, the mother advises her: You are a girl. You have to wear clothes that cover you properly. You have to sit a certain way, with your legs crossed. You cannot be like boys. You have to be aware around boys and men. It is very new to the girl to hear this. But as the mother keeps repeating this often, it starts to become stronger in her, that she is a girl, not a boy. Initially it will be difficult. She will forget. The mother will point out. The child will try to remember the next time. It is not easy. Especially when all the boys are around her are carefree. But with repeated reinforcement of the message, when the child puts in effort sincerely, regularly, it becomes easier. After even further and continuous reinforcements (by herself and from the mother) it becomes ingrained in her that she is a female, and automatically she carries herself accordingly. There is no need for her to remember each time. It is as though it is embedded in every cell of her body that she is a female.

Similarly, if we are able to recollect our true nature by putting so much effort daily, continuously and sincerely, then after a certain period we will reach a point where without any effort we will be able to recognize ourselves as a nameless and formless being. This is how it can happen. If you know any other way, please tell me.

Remembering ourselves always is the Sadhana. If you make the attempt very sincerely, Grace will follow. And to do this practice, you need to be in Surrender. Because when you are in Surrender you will listen to the Master.

Then his words will make you more concentrated towards the goal. Your surrender will help you stay focused on the goal and not get diluted in other activities. Because your effort in this should be highly focused. For focusing on the objective, Surrender helps. It does not mean that you should not do anything and stay idle. Surrender helps you to do the right thing because you have no agenda of your own. The Master guides you as to what to do.

So, first you have to train yourself to be in Surrender. "O Gurunatha, I have surrendered to you totally. I have no agenda of my own, no expectations, no likes, dislikes. Whatever you say, I will do." This way you are dissolving. The second practice is remembering the self, or self-remembering. If you succeed in the first practice, it creates a good atmosphere in you to practice the second one. When you have surrendered, the doors open. The second practice will become much easier. Once you have mastered it, and are established in the nameless, formless nature, then the disciplehood, thinking of you as a person will disappear. Once the disciple has disappeared, where can you find the Master? There is no longer a difference of Master or Disciple. Without Surrender it is extremely difficult. I cannot say it is impossible but there will be tremendous struggles, diversions and a high probability of missing the path. But if you are in surrender, there is no chance for you to lose. Even if you miss the second practice at times you should not miss the first practice. Because only as Surrender increases, your thoughts become much less. Because you have no agenda of your own. You start to disappear. With fewer and fewer oscillations and agitations, it becomes easier to feel your Existence, your true nature as a nameless and formless being. Whoever is able to do both of these is sure to succeed in a shorter period compared to any other path.

Without being in Surrender, if you just practice self-remembrance alone, and straight away try to recall your true nature, there is a high chance that your ego will subtly take over. As you are not in surrender, you will not attract the Master. The Guru's attention will not be turned towards them. They have not served the Master. They have not touched the heart of the Master. Their presence is not registered in the memory of the Master. To reap something, you have to sow something. They become isolated from the zone of the Master. And this is perfect for the ego. The ego will lead them astray. But when you are in Surrender, you are in association with the Master. This association will create opportunities for you to serve the Master in various ways. It does not have to be through money. There are so many ways to serve the Master in surrender mode. This touches the heart of the Master. When you touch the heart of the Master, you can be sure that it is going to help you touch the Truth. Because the Master is nothing but the Truth.

And the Master can give you the experience of the nameless and formless in various ways. He alone can give you glimpses of the Truth. Only after getting these glimpses, can you recollect and remember. Otherwise, what are you going to recollect? Your ego will trick you. So, dedicate yourself totally to this. Otherwise, it is not going to happen. You check within, are you totally dedicated to this practice? You should know if you are dedicated totally or not. This is all about knowing yourself! If you know that you have not dedicated yourself to these two practices (Surrender and Self-Remembering) then take a strong decision. Then do not deviate. If you miss, do not brood. Come right back. Give it your all. Give it your best. Check right now, have you given your best? Life is an opportunity. You have to give your best. The best. Maximum. Totally. Only when you dedicate yourself totally, when you give yourself totally, only then this will happen. 100% has to be given. In all other tasks, if you give 20% effort, you might get less than 20% result, 20% result or more than 20% result. *Someone just buys a lottery and could get a Crore rupees. A student puts in only 40% of effort for an exam. With some luck he could score a high percentage if most of the questions in the exam came from what he studied.* But here, even if you give 99% it won't happen. You have to give yourself 100%. This is the difference. This is the reality. *It is like you have a lot of wealth, but you have secured it some place digitally with a pin number. It is 6 digits. Even if one is wrong, you cannot beg saying, I have 5 digits right, so please give me part of the money. All 6 digits have to be in place or you get nothing. It is like that.* Same thing here. 100%. That is how the system is. That is why it seems very difficult. Because people are not ready to involve themselves, to give themselves. But the formula is simple. This is the main Sutra. It is the Mahasutra. If you want to know yourself, give 100% for these two tasks. Otherwise, your success is simply delayed from birth to birth to birth. And your ego will be fine with it. It has no problem. It will create that attitude in you, 'Why worry? Anyway it will come sometime.' Then you begin to fall.

The good deeds you have done earlier, the blessings of other souls, the blessings of Bhagavan have all brought you here and taught you that a human birth is a great opportunity to know oneself. We should not miss this opportunity. So look within and be honest. See if you are dedicated 100%. The one which is existing here and now as nameless and formless is telling you this Sutra. Only IT can tell you about how you can reach this state which is already existing in you. IT is telling you. This brain is not telling you. It is not a trainer speaking. IT is revealing, how to reach the state which is there (pointing to us).

By 100% involvement in these 2 things.

Then Mahaprabu was silent for some time, after which he said:

Here, (referring to Himself) the harvest is over. The fruit is being enjoyed. You have to try to get the fruit. Don't see how I am living now. Don't see me as this physical form. IT is giving these words to you. The words are the real Master. You are seeing me outside the prison. There is a dance happening. But if you start dancing inside the prison, how will it work? In all other kinds of teachings, the teacher should follow what he teaches. But here the Master is free. You are still bound by karmas and vasanas. What he tells you to do is not something he needs to follow. So don't be cheated by looking at me now. You can imagine my practice days. You are seeing me work so hard for your Jnana imagine how much I would have worked for myself.

December 24th, 2022
Rest House at Paliapattu

The Journey without you

The disciple is on a journey with the Master. For some time, both are traveling. Then, the disciple starts to dissolve, and at one point the disciple disappears. But the Journey continues! This is how it works, says Mahaprabu, while pointing out what the disciple needs to do for his/her part.

It was way past midnight. With Sri Mahaprabu in Samadhi for a long time, maybe 2 hours. He opened his eyes. Told me we could have Tea (which he brought for Satsang!) He then said the following:

You need to disappear. That is the goal. How can you disappear while you still are there? Where are you? In all your efforts, practices, in all expectations, you are there. The Guru keeps on repeating 'Be with Inner Contact, Be Aware of that which is Aware, Keep your attention on the Feeling of Existence in all activities'. Who is listening to it? The Ego. Is there any relationship between Ego and that Feeling of Existence? No. Even though the Ego listens, there is no relationship. Even though the Master keeps on repeating, who listens? The Ego listens. The Ego is paying attention to it.

There are two things here. Ego and Attention. Does the Feeling of Existence relate to Ego or Attention? It is related to Attention, Awareness. So, when the Ego listens to the words: 'Have inner contact on the feeling of Existence', even though that feeling of Existence does not belong to the Ego, one day or the other, the Attention will grab it and take you to that Inner Contact. You cannot do this practice of having an inner contact on the feeling of Existence, with the Ego. But that is how it starts. The Ego pays attention. The Ego is in the frontend. But in the backend, there is Attention. Attention is a part of the Feeling of Existence. So, one day or the other, the Master's words will come straight to the Attention, which will then lead to that Feeling of Existence. Yes, today you are feeling bad that you are not able to perform actions with Inner-Contact. But move on, keep trying. Don't be stuck there. For example, you read a book for 3 hours. You missed the inner contact totally. Now you will feel bad. But don't get stuck. Don't cling to that bad feeling.

So what you need to do first is to be in Surrender. Whatever you tell me Gurunatha, I will do. I will never take back this pledge of Surrender. Then the Guru will start his work. Because the disciple is determined, the Guru will work. Now will the disciple give room to his ego? No. Slowly the Guru will travel with him and put him on the track. Because he has totally given himself to him. But if the disciple has only surrendered partially, the instructions from the Guru also will not be whole. Because he is divided. He is two. Sometimes with the heart, sometimes with the ego. Only when he is whole, when he has totally surrendered, the work can happen. The disciple's attitude should be, 'Dear Master, I have full faith that your goal is only one: To free me from this ignorance, from this identification and establish the Truth in me. So, I have no more questions, no more expectations. Even if things don't appear to go well, it is happening for my eventual benefit. I will follow your words. Please help me.' That is real Surrender. See, I know the system, when and how it works. But only if you follow my words will it happen. So, you have to bring yourself to that mindset.

The Disciple has to be in FULL Surrender for a LONG period. Only then the Doors that Osho talked about will be kept open. [A prolonged silence. Then Mahaprabu asked me to eat another bun if hungry]. So, you should have no doubt as to what to do anymore. Total Surrender. In that Surrender, as much as possible try to be with Inner Contact. Even if you miss Inner Contact, do not ever miss Surrender.

SC: And this negative mindset (I am not able to practice etc.) has to go.

Mahaprabu: Definitely. It will drag you way down. As you stay in Satsang more and more, it will go away. See, it doesn't belong to Atma. So, one day it has to go. We have developed these mindsets. They have to be dropped. A pleasant breeze should flow inside.

[A prolonged silence]

We have been sitting for so many hours here in this small room. Would you be able to sit like this with the wife or children?

SC: Not at all.

Mahaprabu: What have I given you to keep you here in this room? Nothing. Just sitting here gives us confidence, comfort, a feeling that we are actually living, a feeling that these are good moments. That feeling keeps us here.

You need to disappear. I need to take you to that place where you are not. You alone from there (pointing to me) are coming on a journey with me. (Mahaprabu repeated this three times. The 'you' he refers to is personhood, individuality.) You alone, You alone must come with me. And in that journey, you need to disappear, but that journey should continue. This is how it is. In the beginning, you are there, but as you travel, you must disappear and yet the journey continues. For this, only you must be there with me.

SC: You mean just the individuality here with no attachments at all.

Mahaprabu: Yes, just your individuality. Think of it like being an orphan. You must come to this point first. Check for yourself, if you are there now. Only then the real journey will start. When you alone come to me. (Referring to zero mental attachments). Then the journey starts. Until then everything that is happening is preparation for the journey. Preparation for you to be just you.

You can check if you are at that point of total detachment or not. I am telling you how the system works. The journey will start only when that happens. When you alone are there, you are ready to travel with the Guru, and you are ready to disappear. See how important the Guru is. This is a journey unlike any other you have experienced. In all your journeys so far, you were there at the beginning and you were there at the end. This is very different. Here, after a point there will still be travel but without a traveller. That is the very objective of the Journey, for the traveller to disappear. *For example, a man has been riding on a horse in all his travels. Wherever he went, it was on the horse. But there comes a point when he has disappeared, and the horse alone is travelling.* (Laughing).

SC: (Amazed at the aptness of his examples) It makes sense but I cannot conceptualize it, because then I am back on the horse.

Mahaprabu: It can never be conceptualized. See the difficulty. I must have crossed this point myself at one time. Imagine. Otherwise, how can I explain this? That is why you said, 'How is it that as soon as you enter the room and sit, you seem to totally disappear.' It is because the travelling is continuously happening without the traveller here.

SC: So, the flaw is we assume in your case that there is a traveller who came and sat here and then disappeared.

Mahaprabu: The travel alone is happening continuously. [A prolonged silence]

SC: (Thinking how wasted this life has been so far) The ego has been the driver, causing so many accidents. Yet now when I observe it keenly it disappears, it vaporizes.

Mahaprabu: That moment where you see the absence of the ego, needs to be extended. When you keenly observe it vaporizes. And yet something is still existing. Existence continues. You know what vaporized. You also feel what did not vaporize. So, at the moment of vaporization there is a continuity. That continuity should extend.

SC: But a momentum of habit brings the culprit back. And worrying about that, makes the next moments go missed. Further worry.

Mahaprabu: Yes. See, a few years back you did not even have these moments that you feel now. The absence. I told you long ago, when I was driving from Vandavasi. These words came when I was very close to the Rest house. (SC: Amazed at his memory). The one who thinks he is not able to be with Awareness is also a thought. You are identified with that thought. Instead of that, what would be beneficial is to generate a thought that 'Yes, it is possible to try further'. You can be identified with that thought instead. This thought has a totally positive influence. So, the choice makes all the difference. When I brought this to your attention then, you grasped it immediately and said so.

SC: But I have forgotten now.

Mahaprabu: I remember. Worry is a negative thought. Replace it with the second choice. 'I can try. It is possible.' It will make a big difference. Then when the ego disappears and existence is felt, that moment will extend. As it extends more and more, you are going into a new experience. The experience of travelling without that ego. Once that happens, you will see the difference. As easily as an unripe vs. ripe fruit. As easily as salt water vs. drinking water.

SC: So, I need to remember to keep bringing the second choice and not worry about missing.

Mahaprabu: Yes, and where is it possible for that to grow?

SC: When I am in Satsang with the Guru.

Mahaprabu: And where will it not grow?

SC: When I am not with the Guru.

Mahaprabu: Good. So, you understand all this. But if your effort does not match it, if your effort is half-hearted, then your travel with the ego will only increase. If your effort is total, then the feeling of Existence will increase tremendously. As that experience becomes stronger and stronger, the ego experience cannot withstand it. The ego keeps becoming weaker. The Feeling of Existence becomes stronger and stronger. Keep on extending that moment when the ego disappears and you feel Existence. As you keep on increasing it, the Ego cannot even come close at a point. Then it is over.

See the problem clearly. Even though you understand this but still do not implement it totally, what are you doing then? Simply passing the time. You might imagine otherwise. The system is crystal clear. You have to do everything that is needed and at the same time avoid what is not to be done. Write this down clearly: What is needed (being with the Guru in Satsang) should be done. Also, what is not needed should be avoided. There are three possibilities. A is not done but B is done (worst). A is done and B is also done (they cancel out, so no use). The 3rd case alone brings success. A is done and B is not done. (Laughing). You have to do both. So, give tremendous importance to implementing what you have understood. It is simple. You know when you keenly observe it vaporizes. When you let go, it comes back. So, increase those moments of observation. Whatever should be done to increase those moments, do that. Whatever affects those moments, should not be done. If you follow this sincerely, SUCCESS IS INVEITABLE.

OK, give some rest.

December 30th, 2022
Sitthalapakkam House

Unconscious rules the Conscious

In each of us there is the unconscious and the conscious. The strength of the unconscious prevents us from going deeper. It does not cooperate with the conscious portion of the system. Using various examples, Sri Mahaprabu distinguishes the two. He shows how the association with the Master rips apart the unconscious, thereby giving strength to the conscious.

Sri Mahaprabu was in Samadhi for a long time. After which he spoke about what happens to that last thought before going into Samadhi.

Just before entering into Samadhi, I might have wanted to say something. That thought would have been at a bud stage but didn't come out. After a long time, it might come. But there is no identification with it. It would be like a star nearby in space. Because that body (mental) is different from this body (physical). Even though the physical body consciousness goes, the subtle body consciousness is still there, but it doesn't disturb me. That single thought will come to the attention and stand in front: Boss, you started this thought, but it hasn't processed it. Here it is. Would you like to do anything with it? It is something like that. I don't even have to reply. The fact that I didn't reply makes it go away. And it goes away like a meteor (Mahaprabu enacted how fast it goes away)

SC: After that, there won't be a memory of it either?

Mahaprabu: There will be a memory of it because we are still conscious. In fact, it will be stronger in memory since there isn't a cluster of thoughts. Just one thought. So it will be strong. *If a 1,000 people came to your marriage you won't remember most of them. But if only 1 person came to your wedding. Imagine!!* (Laughing). But even that thought won't be a disturbance.

So in the entire one hour, there will be no thoughts. In rare cases one or two thoughts. Even those, when they come and go, you are again in THAT.

SC: For this (Mahaprabu encourages us to not use words like "I" or "Me"), in an hour, there are gaps of thoughtlessness, surrounded by thoughts or the idea of an attempter trying something.

Mahaprabu: That itself is a great blessing. It is good. With continued practice, those gaps will pierce, tear and open up avenues.

Because, your brain has to cooperate. For example, you told me that yesterday some people from the bank met with you. At that time Mahaprabu called you. He could sense that he could not penetrate you. Because your mindset is 'I am engaged with some important discussion.' At that time you won't receive, even though you know the importance of Mahaprabu's call. Your brain is like that. At that time, all the other doors are closed by you. It is just a habit. Imagine a more serious meeting, where you have an appointment with a very famous doctor regarding an issue in your body. See how tightly all other doors will be closed. So, for such a brain, getting even a small gap of rest is good. The pattern of the brain's thinking must change. As you meditate more and more it will change. You have to keep on working on it. See, your involvement in mediation is based on what? That inner system, the current mindset. With that you are consciously involving meditation. Even though you are sitting in meditation, the unconscious is still very active. That's why your gaps are small. The unconscious still has a lot of strength. You have to cross the unconscious to go to the super-conscious state. But it is a great start.

How the process works

As you consciously involve more in Dhyanam and Satsang, the unconscious will start to exhaust itself, especially if you are not strengthening it in worldly outward activities. For example, take a situation unrelated to Satsang. (some outward activity). Now your conscious is there. Say the unconscious also has priority for that task. Since both unconscious and conscious like this avenue, the unconscious will use the conscious and keep you engaged there. Without your knowing, you will be sucked into it. Now come back to the current situation of meditation. Initially there is a mismatch between conscious and unconscious. Conscious wants to meditate. The Unconscious has latent energy to go outward and will drag you out. There is a lack of alignment, a cooperation. Since your meditation is a disturbance for the Unconscious (It wonders... why is this guy starting to sit quietly now? (laughing)). But as you increase your time in meditation and satsang, the unconscious will slowly lose its energy. Where does that energy go? To the Conscious! Now there is a match. Both are aligned towards the same path. When all the energy has been depleted in the unconscious, it will disappear. Now the super-conscious which is behind, will be felt by the conscious. Then things will fall in line. This is how the process happens.

That's why we should consciously make the effort to attend Satsang regularly and do Dhyanam regularly. This alone will disturb the Unconscious and weaken it. You can understand all this because you have experienced it. Otherwise, your unconscious will be the listener and it will be a waste.

Back to the bank example, there your conscious and unconscious were both engaged with the bankers. When Mahaprabu called, he sensed this, even though you did not tell him they were with you. So there was no further talk from his side. That is how IT operates. Right now also the unconscious is there in you, but it has no priority. It is weak. Whenever it is weak, the Guru will act really fast (Laughing!!!). That is his chance! And if the disciple is really angry. Imagine. The conscious itself will become unconscious! All the doors will be closed. Guru won't even attempt to enter. This is how the system is. Power is given to the conscious and the unconscious. That is how the game is. The Guru needs tremendous patience.

For example, a male sucks a female breast in the act of sex. What is he getting out of it? Nothing is secreted. Nothing is actually transferred. So who is in total control? The Unconscious. Because as a child, it sucked milk. How? Unconsciously. The child did not know anything about the breast or milk. Hunger arose. Instinctively it got the milk from the breast. This was recorded strongly in the unconscious. During sex, when the unconscious takes over, it relives the deeply ingrained satisfaction from the act of sucking.

SC: Then why is there the sense of joy in sex?

Mahaprabu: Yes, as a child too when you got the milk, the happiness was recorded along with the act. The quality of happiness (X) is the same. When the pangs of hunger were satisfied, X was recorded. During sex too, that X is felt. When you eat a sweet also there is happiness felt right? It is the same X, just that the concentration is less. *It is like adding less salt, more salt and more salt. The concentration is different but salt is salt.* So what you are calling sex is more X! Why does there appear to be more happiness in sex? Because you are giving additional conscious qualifiers such as looks, colour, touch etc. And there are hormones coming into play.

SC: But women also suck the breast of mothers. How come they don't have that craving later?

Mahaprabu: The record is there for a female also. When a male sees a female, he notices the breast even if it is covered and hidden, and never revealed in public. The memory keeps getting kindled. But for a woman, it is just a part of her body. Flesh. It is not even her primary sexual organ. Also, her attention is towards the male body naturally. That is how it is designed. But when her breast is touched during sex, that unconscious record of her having sucked milk comes back strongly. Even though she doesn't suck, the stored joy is evoked. It is a very complex mechanism.

The point is to show you how the unconscious can take you over totally, just in the act of a mouth sucking a piece of flesh. And the joy that you experience is nothing but a tiny ray of the Atma Sugam (Happiness of Atma). It reveals a small glimpse of itself. This is all a play, the Leela of Brahman, that Supreme Power. That is why a Jnani does not see anyone as a sinner. Where are you to commit a sin? That's why the Gita says, the Lord alone is doing it all. And that Atma cannot be killed.

But the Guru is very careful not to reinforce this Advaitic attitude on a disciple early on. Because without his knowledge, his ego will misuse it. Under the pretext that everything is One, or everything is a dream, it will exploit him to chase external happiness. Soon he will be giving talks to a group of followers who garland him. And the intelligence is so much, that he will do it consciously. Not that he does it innocently. And there won't be anyone to question him, since already he is teaching others. But if he does that in the presence of a Guru, the Guru will simply say: What if I slap you now, or pour some boiling water on your thigh? See if you can take it as a dream. If you can take it peacefully, you are a Jnani. So many people are pretending to be like a Jnani. They have forgotten when this pattern of thinking got into them in the first place. The Unconscious has taken over the Conscious, which now cleverly operates.

For example, a doctor performs an operation to remove a kidney. Is that a conscious or unconscious act?

SC: Conscious.

Mahaprabu: Another doctor, especially in India, is in the business of selling organs like kidneys illegally. Is that conscious or unconscious?

SC: The unconscious has taken the conscious over in him.

Mahaprabu: See how well the example fits. All ethics will go into the background. You will frame your own ethics. Especially if wealth and fame accrue. Mahaprabu has seen so many in this pattern, and where they ended up in life. It all started with spirituality! So either, naturally you should have a very strong goal that I only want to know myself, or you should be with a living Master. The former is very rare.

All this explanation is to show you why the Guru doesn't tell the disciple that everything is a Leela, a play. Because there are so many traps waiting. That's why Buddha never spoke about the Leela. He even said, if you want to know the truth, be with me quietly for two years. No questions.

So when you are in satsang with a real master, he will help the conscious in you to take over the unconscious and tear it. When you are with a teacher or fake master, it is the unconscious operating on both sides. A real master will immediately see it and catch it when a disciple is dominated by the unconscious. That is why a Master is so important. And this is where Surrender is a huge help. Only when you are in Surrender will you allow the Master to reduce the strength of your Unconscious. See, the Conscious is weak in a disciple and the Unconscious is strong due to years, janmas (life-times) of habit. Using this weak conscious, you have to drag the Unconscious down. It is like, *making a cat pull an elephant.* But keep on doing it in Surrender and one day the unconscious will dissolve into a cat. The elephant (Conscious) will simply trample the cat. Today we have to be extremely careful since the Unconscious is the elephant that can trample the cat (Conscious).

And when you interact with others who are unconscious, your unconscious will immediately multiply. You will instantly forget the Guru. He knows. The disciple has forgotten. He has taken on so much more unconscious energy. This is why solitude is so important.

See how IT is giving you. How can you understand all this in a book? It is a very big system. Not complicated. Just Elephant and Cat! But with this system see how the whole world is operating.

SC: How strongly we feel we are an individual. That I am Formless is hard to fathom unless I consciously become aware. It should be natural but it isn't. That's how powerful the unconscious is.

Mahaprabu: Yes. With continuous effort, continuous effort it is definitely possible. For instance, right now if you take regular life, what will the unconscious be doing? (It was somewhere past 3 AM when we were talking).

SC: Sleeping.

Mahaprabu: But what are we doing? Not letting it sleep. In this way we are making the slave weak. Just the fact that you are awake now, is strength to the Conscious. We are saying NO to the Unconscious. It is there in the background, noticing that 'This guy is ignoring me daily and sitting up all night.' (Every day for the last few weeks, we have been in Satsang from around 10 PM to 4 or 5 AM). See, I am not planning this at all for us to stay up all night each time. The system is doing it. If the Super-Conscious makes me lie down and stay at Anbu mayyam (Mahaprabu's residence), what will you do? We won't be here. In all your previous trips this did not happen. The Super-Conscious is the Master, who is acting behind the Conscious and Unconscious play. Imagine, He rules the Unconscious! How powerful He is. Paramahamsa called it Kali, who plays kites in the sky. Only a few kites get cut and escape into the sky while all cheer. *Avan andri oru anuvum asayadhu. Without him even one atom will not move.* So powerful IT is. IT decides whether this satsang right now is happening or not. I did not plan to stay up all night and keep you up all night to weaken your unconscious.

SC: So, in you, there is only Conscious. No Unconscious.

Mahaprabu: (Immediately) Super Conscious alone. Nothing else. There isn't anything else. Only the Boss and this body as His instrument. He operates this body. That is why the brain here is always relaxed. If something happens, it is His order. If something did not happen, it is His order too. That it did not happen, also happened. It happened by His grace too. So, nothing here is affected either way. All happens by His grace alone, is the thought that is recorded.

SC: For us, we have an expectation that it should happen 'This way', which creates all the problems.

Mahaprabu: Laughing. Yes. That your body is alive for some more duration, is itself an event that is happening.

Mahaprabu laughed for a long time.

━━━━━ ◈ ◂◂ ◆ ▸▸ ◈ ━━━━━

January 3rd, 2023
Sitthalapakkam House. Past 3 AM.

Moment to Moment Practice

We are continuously feeding wrong information to the brain. So, the entire life is lived on this wrong basis. Hence the suffering. Sri Mahaprabu spoke about what we need to do from the moment of waking, throughout the day, and how Satsang with the Master is the biggest help.

A disciple using his feet, moved the cloth he was sitting on. Sri Mahaprabu caught it.

At each and every moment we are here, we should use it for our practice. See, even while moving that cloth. You just moved that cloth with your feet. It happened quickly. Even in that small movement, there should be an Awareness of that action. An Awareness of who moved it.

What makes the body function? Existence. You can feel this Existence. With attention on this feeling of Existence, you can observe the body moving the cloth. Now both the outer task and inner task are happening. You are not lost in identification. This is the only thing we need to remember. As soon as you remember the feeling of Existence, it will come to you instantly. You don't need to bring it from the Himalayas.

How the brain records information

There is a cloth. That body moved the cloth aside using the feet. But that happened without the inner contact. That's why I asked him, whether he has done it with inner contact. He said 'No'. If you do it without the inner contact, what do you think the brain is recording? 'I am sitting. I want some space so I am moving the cloth aside'. This is what it records. Here the 'I am' refers to what? It is the problem. The brain records 'I am an individual. I am a male. I need some space so I am moving the cloth.' So, unconsciously the 'I am' is connected with the body. It is a totally wrong record. But even such a small action has strengthened that wrong idea even more. Imagine how all our actions strengthen it. But really it is a wrong record. The meaning for 'I am' which is recorded, is wrong. If you see the record closely, in 'I want the space, so I am moving the cloth' the record is one of an individual. But if the action is done with inner contact, then the record is this: 'As the body needs the space, I am moving the cloth using the body, using the legs.' This is the right record. Here 'I' refers to the feeling of

Existence, or Atma. If you have the inner contact, this will be the record. Now the right information is stored. If you follow this in every action, especially small actions, then the right information will be recorded. Now that will be strengthened. In due course of time, you can try feeling the inner contact even with complex activities. Then you elevate the practice to critical situations.

What is non-doership?

The strength you have built will give you the remembrance of who you are and which is doing the action. Actions will happen and you will be separate from the action and activity. And you will see the situation very clearly. This is the absence of doership. No karmas will bind you. There is no tension. As you are in a flow, you will not worry about the consequences either. It is an integrated flow. A complete flow. You are a part. You have moved something one step in this flow. So, neither are you the doer nor the owner.

The right information that is recorded about the 'I' will keep you always in phase with the universal flow. No deviation. There will be a harmony. Because there is no separate 'I'. Only a single force. Not a fragmented force. As you are always in the flow, you will always feel the harmony. You will feel a silence always. You will not cling on to anything anywhere.

Actually, even now you are still in the flow and there is harmony. But due to the false record in the brain you are unable to recognize and realize the harmony. Even then, when you try to go inside and establish the inner contact, you feel the silence. Because the harmony is already established. The silence is already there. We are not bringing it from outside each time. Just that due to the wrong record in the brain we have become insensitive to the harmony. We are unable to sense it even though it is present. But with effort we can sense it. So, we have to keep preparing ourselves to sense it. **Sensing the harmony continuously, thereby remaining in silence is called Self-Realization.** In every activity, you must not lose the inner contact. Do things in a relaxed manner. While walking, while doing some chores, while doing any activity where we are not answerable to others, you should practice this sincerely.

The benefit of Satsang

In the very first chapter of Final Talks, Annamalai Swami speaks about the importance of this practice. We are practicing here every weekend during Satsang, to realize the stream which is flowing inside. To realize the inner contact. And every weekend we are trying to erase the false information. By frequent meditation in these two days, we are trying to give the right information to the brain. After this, we have to go back and perform our activities using the strength obtained during the weekend. We have to rectify the mistakes as we see them happening. Then more strengthening on the weekend can be done. Again putting it more into practice during the week. This will reduce the frequency of mistakes. For that to be reduced we should be very conscious here (in Satsang on weekends). We are totally disconnecting from the world for these two days. We are sitting here with the only purpose of getting the inner connection and recording the right information. If you don't do this sincerely here every weekend, then during the week since you have not developed the strength, you will make more mistakes. You will not realize the harmonious state. You will not be in silence. You will suffer.

Just sitting every weekend to practice this is not a natural thing. Bodies are designed for activities. Just sitting and doing this is not a natural flow. It is kind of a stagnation. Nature has given you all special permission. 'OK. You have asked for this. You have deserved it. Now go and sit. Feel who you really are. Correct the record.' Instead, if you waste this golden opportunity given to you by Nature week after week, Nature will withdraw. You can try to come back to Satsang, but Nature won't allow it. You will quickly be dragged into Karmas. The situations around you will change. Even if you try to fight it and come here, you cannot win over Nature. You will soon lose the energy to fight and succumb to the karmas given to you by Nature. You will give up. You will be dragged into Karmas. So, it is very important to realize that you have been granted special permission. This is a privilege. Realize the purpose and put in a total sincere effort.

With thoughts too

Just like acting without inner contact, we also think without inner contact. The speed of action is much less compared to the speed of thinking. If you miss the inner contact in bodily actions, how can you catch it in the thinking process? It is too fast. That too, for normal thoughts on a normal day. Imagine if there was a major event in your house this morning. Like a wedding. From the moment you wake up you would be fully identified and will act on the basis of the ego alone. There is not even a gap for the inner contact to enter.

What to do?

So, each and every day, wake up slowly, with inner contact. Observe. All night I didn't see or feel anything outside. Now they are felt and seen. Who is watching? The eyes? No. A blind man has eyes too. Beyond the eyes, something is seeing out through the eyes. What is that? It is that which even gave me the information that I have woken up. It is as though IT has entered the body, woken it up and is looking out. This has to be practiced and felt daily, in a slow manner. Then your day will start correctly. Then focus on the inner contact in all the bodily movements. As the body gets up to a sitting, then standing position, as it walks to the bathroom, as it brushes its teeth, as it washes, in all these activities have the inner contact so that there is no identification with the body which is doing its activities. Only then can you apply this practice to thoughts too.

The master with the body cannot always come with all disciples, and be with them in all their activities.

[At this point a disciple said 'The Master can help from inside too'].

Yes. For that, you need to be highly receptive and stay tuned with the Master. When you are in Surrender with the Master, sincerely practicing what he is saying and progressing in your Sadhana, then because of your love for him and your service, a communion happens. Then the Master, who is really formless, can help the disciple be aware whenever he misses. When all your actions are towards serving the Master with love and dedication for him, and not for your ego, then there is a connection. It was there between Bhagavan and Annamalai Swami. He worked only and only for Bhagavan. He had no personal interests. Seeing that, Bhagavan started loving him. That love formed a bridge. No matter where Annamalai Swami was, Bhagavan always had him in his consciousness. For example, Bhagavan would feel, 'OK he is in the building works now. He should not miss the inner contact.' Such a wish from Bhagavan would go to the universe and directly touch the disciple and have its effect. In that way, a Master can help. But for that, the disciple must deserve it. He should make himself eligible. Only then will it happen. And this is applicable not only with the Master in the form. If you love God directly, and honestly do all your actions for God alone, then God will help in the same way too.

When you start to know who you are, you are moving towards real freedom. Which means you can decide. If you want to come again with a body, you can. If you don't want to you will not. But first, you have to come to this point of total freedom.

[Then Sri Mahaprabu remarked]

It is so hard to translate the flow that is coming moment to moment, into English. The brain has to receive it (in Tamil), translate it, make sure there are no grammatical mistakes and then deliver it through the mouth. The flow may not wait for all this! It keeps coming. We should capture it as it comes. Like a fish entering a net. (laughing) So please all of you learn Tamil!

January 22nd, 2023
Rest House at Paliapattu

Correcting the Ego

Nature has a built-in mechanism in us to sense when we are with ego. Sri Mahaprabu found that early on. He shared an example of how he would correct himself in daily activities, and spoke about the necessity for a new lifestyle if we are to achieve our goal of knowing ourselves.

Weekend Satsang just started. It was around 9:30 PM. Sri Mahaprabu had driven from Chennai to Tiruvannamalai just like he has been doing for over 10 years now, without missing a weekend. Looking at the disciple who is responsible for the kitchen he said the following:

When you are able to do the entire cooking with love, without any irritation, throughout the process, then meditation will come to you automatically. This is especially true in cooking. Simply sitting for meditation will cheat you. People even get irritated if they can't sit and meditate. See how foolish that is.

Correcting the ego in real-life

[Then Sri Mahaprabu reminisced about his days as a disciple of Swami Thiruvadithuli as to how he would correct his ego in real-life situations – It was a great lesson for us]

After Satsang, I used to sit to eat in the first batch, since I would be hungry and also was worried that if I sat later, the food might be finished. At least some items always would be done in the first round. But I distinctly felt this inside me as wrong. So, I made it a policy to serve first and eat last. Serving is not easy. You have to wait till the last person eats. You will notice the food depleting. Some items may not even be there for you. You have to see what each one likes and serve accordingly. Then you have to clear the leaf of each person. Initially, it was disgusting. Touching someone's leftovers. The leaf tears. The liquid spills out. Then I decided to bring a bucket with me to help with the task. And you have to do all this without the slightest expectation of admiration from others. I used to clean the entire floor with water, then wipe it and make sure it dries, so we could serve the next batch of devotees. This became regular. After 2 years of this, one day a lady came to me after the service. All the food was depleted. I had served it all. But she came to me and said, 'I have been watching you each time. You serve everyone and only in the end do you eat. That too, whatever little is left over. Come eat now.' But I knew there was hardly any food left. Still, she asked me to sit. It turns out she had kept a little of each dish for me. She served me that food, with so much love. Till today I have not eaten a meal served with so much love. I had tears in my eyes. She stayed till the end and served me alone. Everyone had left. That is when I experienced that the happiness in giving is much more than the happiness in getting.

We sense the ego

I'm telling you this to show you that wherever you sense the ego in you, there you have to get down and work. I used to sit first to eat, worrying that the food may be done. The beauty of life is that life shows whenever you are with ego. Everyone knows this for themselves. In other words, if there is a block in the flow due to the ego, each of us knows there is a block. We are made aware automatically. We should be thankful for that. Nature has given that knowledge to sense this. We may not know how to remove the block, or show interest in removing the block. But we know there is a block. Imagine if it didn't show you. You won't even try to remove it. Those who are interested in removing the block, they alone get the flow. If you just follow this, there is no need of a Master. If you ask me who is the Master, our honesty to life is the Master. We know when we are not right. Even though we know that we are not right, we are not ready to make ourselves right. That is not right. As we are not right, everything is going in the wrong direction!

It is a feeling that we get when we do something wrong. It is not a thought. Nature has given us this. When you do something right, there is no turbulence felt in you. But if you do something wrong, you feel it instantly. Just like how a dog can trace its way back to an owner just by his smell. Similarly, God has given us his smell this way. That alone is enough for you to retrace yourself to him. Why is it easy for a dog and not a human being? Because the dog depends on smell alone. And it compares the owner's smell with other smells on the way. Even if it comes across the boss's clothes, it knows that is not the boss. Even though the smell is close to that of the Master. It will move on. Only when it finds its Master, will it stop searching. Till then it will keep on searching.

But we forget the basic smell, the reference smell. And the thinking process comes in the way. We start thinking. When we start thinking we miss the feeling. That's why in spirituality, all the masters are saying 'Stop

Thinking'. Thinking is a hindrance. It is not useful and it is a hindrance. The feeling is important. The smell.

A new lifestyle is needed

Living with an enlightenment about Godliness can be achieved only by living a particular lifestyle. It is not a sitting, doing and finding affair. It is a lifestyle. So the lifestyle that can lead us to enlightenment about Godliness should be learned and adopted. For that, we need a Master. To show you the lifestyle that leads to enlightenment. Both for attaining it and maintaining it.

Buddha says: If you want to attain enlightenment, stay with a living Master. If it is not possible, live with the seekers of Truth. If that too is not possible, then live in solitude. Why? Because only then you can have a particular lifestyle. It is very important to kncw that enlightenment is possible only if you live a particular lifestyle. For learning and living in that way, you need a Master. For example, if the particular Lifestyle is L, and everyone has L1, L2, L3 etc, all those lifestyles should be changed towards L. It should merge with L. How to spend 24 hours, how to spend a week, how to spend a month, a year, an entire life in L. In the beginning with time consciousness, but in the end without time consciousness. Does not mean unconsciously. So you start with time and end in timeless. Starting with limit and ending with limitless. Starting with restlessness and ending in rest.

January 28th, 2023
Rest House at Paliapattu

Body vs. Form

Sri Mahaprabu urged us to stop using the phrase or instruction 'I am not the body' and instead use 'I am not the form.' The latter, naturally leads to the Formless. A simple change but very effective.

An important correction is needed in our understanding. We know we should not get identified with the body. Now we should correct it by saying we should not get identified with form. This makes a big difference when you bring it into practice. Form and body are the same. But the word makes the difference. Try it and you will see the difference. Hereafter consciously think that we should not get identified with the form. Only when you think this way, will you have the interest to seek the Formless. On the other hand, if you think we should not get identified with the body, then what to seek? The mode doesn't shift to seeking.

When you stop identifying with form, you will stop identifying with this form and other forms. And if you think not to identify with form, then at the bottom there is a mode that can seek the Formless. Because the Formless is available underneath already. So the attitude is 'I should not focus on the form, so where should I focus? The Formless'. Because it is the Formless that is focusing on the form. Our goal is attentiveness. We are instructing, 'Don't give attention to the form'. Since this instruction is sent to attentiveness, immediately the attention will go to the Formless. So practically, 'I am not the Body' is an instruction that does not work. So instruct properly, 'We should not focus on forms.' Then it is possible to focus on the Formless. Make a correction in your thinking process.

See, the Formless is focusing on the form. The brain is giving the instruction to the Formless 'Don't focus on the form.' Now the attention will realize this and make the correction. Then the attention will turn towards the Formless. Then the strength of the 'I' will get reduced. If you simply practice, 'I am not the body', you are not telling the brain where to focus. So, the identification with body only gets stronger. The ego only increases. That's why spiritual people are angrier than normal people. I'm seeing this. Spiritual people have stronger egos than ordinary people.

From now consciously instruct your brain: We should not focus on the form. Slowly this instruction will be understood by the Formless. Even though the instruction is received by the brain (form) indirectly we are giving it to the Formless. As the subject is about the form, the Formless will consider it. Only the Formless can know about form. The instruction is very clear to it. Unlike the 'I am not the body' instruction. Then it will get awakened. Some extra familiarity is there.

Try it and see. The words are similar: Body and Form. But the effect is very different. See the difference between: 'You are not the body' vs. 'You are not this form'. In the former, the question 'who I am' does not arise. But in the latter, the subsequent question arises, which leads you to the Truth. If I am not this form, then what is my form? This is the right question, which leads you to the Truth. The right question matters. Anyone can ask questions. Anyone who found the solution to anything, must have asked the right question. Intelligence is asking the right questions. Intelligence is in-built. It cannot be borrowed. You cannot lose it. But you might not use it! Everyone has this intelligence. Even an ant. The quality is the same. If all the senses available in us are given to an ant, then an ant will become a human. The intelligence that comes out would be different. So, the difference is in the manifestation. The intelligence is the same from ant to elephant. We should respect that intelligence.

See, a Formless intelligence is existing throughout the world. That's why the earth rotates at a specific angle Why? That's the intelligence. Why an elliptical orbit? Why not circular? That is intelligence. A formless intelligence is existing everywhere. And the same formless intelligence is able to understand why it is not circular! (laughing). A scientist (vijnani) finds out about a specific area of the universe. A Jnani knows the whole. No award or forum can understand the intelligence behind a Jnani. And once a scientist finds something, he immediately expresses everything he knows. A Jnani will not express anything. He enjoys it. When you experience and enjoy it, then moment to moment you are feeling that intelligence. Thus, they are not interested in expressing it like a scientist. They are enjoying it.

Sri Mahaprabu then spoke about wanting to learn other languages, but the time for that can be spent talking to a disciple. Even though Maunam (Silence) is the best language, i.e., Silence alone can communicate love. Silence is the best language. Words corrupt. They immediately dilute the essence. Like a flower in a garden versus a flower tied in a garland. The latter has no life current. Same flower, but big difference. Like that is Silence vs.

Words. But people need to be in a certain state to communicate via Silence. Till then words are necessary. We have to start with the garland, then show the plucked flowers, and then the garden. We have to start from the marketplace. Start with the garland and end in the garden.

✦ ◄◄ ◆ ►► ✦

January 28th, 2023
Rest House at Paliapattu

Seeker visits Mahaprabu

A seeker after having heard about Sri Mahaprabu, visited the Rest house. These are always interesting and valuable to watch, the meeting of a person seeing Sri Mahaprabu for the first time.

As soon as Satsang started, Sri Mahaprabu was quiet. Soon he seemed to drift into Samadhi. It lasted over an hour. He then used the washroom and sat down. Looking at the new visitor and smiling, he said:

Mahaprabu: You can ask something if you want.

Seeker (S): Are you Awakened?

Mahaprabu: Laughing. No Doubt.

S: Asking again. Maybe he didn't understand the accent of Mahaprabu.

Mahaprabu: No doubt! In your terms, what do you mean by Awakening? I would like to know.

S: After thinking a bit, gave some definition. Wasn't audible.

Mahaprabu: Laughing more. Yes, no doubt. Unless and otherwise you realize the state of Awakening, you cannot judge others as to whether they are Awakened or not. So even though you have asked a question and I have given you an answer, you cannot verify it! (Laughing). But in order to keep your mind quiet I have answered your question (Laughing). But it is possible to verify. Once you reach that state, or when you are in association with me for a long time then you will be able to sense whether I have Awakened or not. At first sight, you cannot decide. In due course of time in association with me, then in different situations, you will have an opportunity to understand whether I have awakened or not. That is the only way.

S: Your disciples, are they Awakened?

Mahaprabu: They are in the process. They are in the process. It will take its own time. Different fruits get ripened at different times.

S: You followed Sri Annamalai Swami's teachings, correct?

Mahaprabu: Whatever the questions the seekers ask, I answer. All the teachings that come from me, are coming from my own experience. Not from others. But I know about Annamalai Swami very well. From 1993 I started knowing about him. I used to go to his ashram, his samadhi, continuously from 1997. He helped me a lot. He helped me a lot. In his Samadhi I used to sit for a long time those days. He had written all the important advice given by Bhagavan in the form of songs, on the walls of his Samadhi Shrine (The verses from Ulladu Narpadu were painted on the walls). Even after his samadhi, the paintings were there. Now they have been erased.

S: What was the key teaching of Annamalai Swami?

Mahaprabu: His key teaching was: Don't get identified with the body. You are not a thought. You are not the body. You are Atma. So don't go behind worldly affairs and be sincere to the words of the Master. These are his key advice.

S: Yes, I have read the book Final Talks. Why is his teaching different from that of Bhagavan?

Mahaprabu: Annamalai Swami's teachings were not different from Bhagavan's. He always stressed what Bhagavan taught. Additionally, he gave information about how he served Bhagavan and how Bhagavan trained him. But he never deviated from Bhagavan's teachings.

S: Bhagavan said: You should not meditate on 'I am Brahman'. But Annamalai Swami said: Meditate on 'I am the Self'.

Mahaprabu: Yes. See, searching for Who I am is different. Meditating that I am Brahman is different. That's why Bhagavan didn't stress meditating on 'I am Brahman'. What Annamalai Swami says is, before meditating that you are the Self, first try to know who you are, as per the advice of Bhagavan. After knowing who you are, let us say that is the Self, now you meditate on the Self. But some people without understanding this, without doing the introspection, straight away will sit and meditate 'I am Brahman, I am Brahman' without knowing about it. (Laughing).

S: What are your key teachings?

Mahaprabu: My key teaching is Surrender. See, it is also the key teaching of Bhagavan, but he did not express it explicitly. Because, if Bhagavan did not want Surrender, he would have advised Annamalai Swami from the beginning: 'You have to go inside and do enquiry as to whether you are the body or thought or something beyond. You do this daily. My blessings will follow you.' Bhagavan could have said so. But what actually happened when

Annamalai Swami came to him eager to do meditation? Bhagavan sent him to go and supervise the construction work. Three different times he sent him out. Annamalai Swami only wanted to meditate. And meditate on what? The key teaching of Bhagavan, which as people think, is Self-Enquiry. But Bhagavan's response was 'Go and check how many workers have come. Are they constructing the wall correctly?' He didn't allow him to sit. Because Bhagavan understood, knew that here was a young lad who would become a very good disciple who had a good chance of being enlightened. So, we have to bring him in the path of Surrender, because only in the path of Surrender can the ego be easily lost. So, Bhagavan selected him as his disciple. Now he started training him in the path of Surrender. But he didn't say so explicitly that 'You should follow the path of Surrender, even though I am recommending Self-Enquiry for all.' He knew that Annamalai Swami was a mature disciple and that Surrendering was the way. That was the talent of Bhagavan.

See, the ego will never be ready to surrender in the beginning. So many would come to see Bhagavan. They all had their own egos. Some have an ego with their education, some with their wealth etc. Different kinds of egos. Some positive egos, such as 'I am superior'. Some negative egos like, 'I am not worth anything.' Bhagavan was able to sense all these egos. If he had said, 'If all of you want to attain enlightenment, you must all surrender at my feet. I will guide you personally', no one would have surrendered. Because their egos would make them think 'Why should I surrender and become a slave? I came to this spiritual path because I wanted to be free. Already I am a slave in the world to so many things and relationships. I am looking to come out of it. But the Master is asking me to again become a slave. He wants us to become slaves.'

This way, no ego will surrender. See, the ego wants to achieve something. It wants a challenge. Bhagavan in his great wisdom knew all this very clearly. He listened to all their intellectual questions and said 'Yes, all your questions are right but put them aside and tell me who is the one that has this question.' Now their ego is engaged in the challenge. 'Bhagavan is asking the right question. Now using our intelligence, we need to find the right answer.' Thus, they started working. But how long could one work on this enquiry? One hour? Then more questions. Again, a similar response from Bhagavan. Again they try the enquiry method. Those who were persistent and kept coming back to Bhagavan. It was a kind of filtering. By asking the same question, he ensured that only the real aspirants like Sri Annamalai Swami, Sri Sadhu Om, Sri Papaji, only those seekers who were really sincere in knowing the Truth could stay with Bhagavan for a long time. This duration, this extended time, was enough for Bhagavan to make them surrender at his feet. So silently, the agenda put forward in the foreground was Self-Enquiry, but the background was always Surrender. As they lived with Bhagavan they felt the love of Bhagavan, how he worked, how he lived joyfully. All these things were understood by those who stayed with him patiently. Thus, Bhagavan created enough time by way of teaching self-enquiry as the main method but in the background, he made the disciple surrender.

Bhagavan himself said 'Everybody wants Moksha (liberation) but when I ask them to give themselves to me, they refuse. Then how can Moksha be attained'. What is this but Surrender?

When Annamalai Swami first met Bhagavan, he told him: 'All I want is enlightenment. I am willing to do whatever you say.'

S: How did Bhagavan know that Annamalai Swami was ready for Surrender?

Mahaprabu: Bhagavan did not expressly say that even to Annamalai Swami. He made it happen in the process of staying with him.

S: Described his experience with self-enquiry, the books he read and the teachers he is currently with. He finally came to the conclusion that he was only getting frustrated and, in the end, just wanted to Be, Be, Be. He went on for some time. He spoke for some time.

[We were amazed by the patience of Sri Mahaprabu.]

Mahaprabu: You are asking whether just Being will help with Awakening. If you are really in the state of Beingness, you are Awakened. That itself is the state of Awakening. You may have an idea about what Awakening is, based on reading some books etc.

S: Again, spoke at length about various Gurus/teachers he had met and his experiences, his mind, his reactions etc.

Mahaprabu: Whatever you have said so far has explained your background. Right now, here, put your question to me in simple words: What exactly do you want?

S: I also know that if I want something, I am expecting something, and that will never be the way to awaken. As Ramana said, 'It will never be achieved through willpower.'

[He went on for some time. Mahaprabu continued to listen.]

Mahaprabu: You are telling me you want to get Awakened. So you should know what is the meaning of Awakening. Only then can you expect it.

S: But I should not expect anything, because expectation is of the mind.

Mahaprabu: Yes, but without any expectation no movement, no progress or process will happen. In the beginning, your expectations must be appreciated. So, put all your experiences and learnings regarding awakening aside and tell me. Now at present what is your question?

S: Continued further about the awakened state, etc.

Mahaprabu: I want to really help you. From that angle, I am asking you. Put aside all the concepts about awakening. You are here now. A body is sitting on a stand (chair). You know you are here, correct? Now you ask me what you want. It should be your answer.

S: Be liberated.

Mahaprabu: Wonderful. This is coming from your own words. You want to be liberated. OK. If you want to be liberated, it shows that you feel imprisoned. Tell me from what you want liberation.

S: From all this. Everything.

Mahaprabu: You have beautifully answered 'I want to get liberated.' It shows that you are pressured and imprisoned by something. What is that? Why do you want liberation?

S: [Struggling to answer]

Mahaprabu: No concepts should go into your mind. Just answer the question directly.

S: To get rid of this whole business.

Mahaprabu: You close your eyes, and without using any words observe your answer 'To get rid of...' My question is to get rid of what? Close your eyes and in a relaxed way have a look inside – What you want to get rid of? Then check and confirm if that's the real answer. Feel it. Don't think. Please don't open the eyes. Then verbalize it to me.

S: I want to get rid of the body.

Mahaprabu: You want to get rid of the body? If that is your answer (Seeker confirmed) Then the only way is that you have to commit suicide. (Seeker said something and Mahaprabu continued) But clearly you are not ready for that. It shows that the body is not the real trouble to you. If the body really gave continuous trouble to you, gave you pressure to get rid of it, then you will not ask anyone. You have the freedom to kill the body. But as you are not ready for that, it shows that the body is not giving any pressure to be rid of. It is simply sitting. Obeying all your orders. You ordered it to drive the vehicle to come here. Now you are here. So, it is not the body. Now you move a bit inward. Now you are giving me your own answers. Good.

Don't worry about all the experiences you had in satsangs and the books you have read. You are here. I am here. I am asking you about your problem. You are describing it from your own experience. Only then can you get the right solution. The body is not giving trouble to you. The body is not asking about Liberation and all. Something else inside is asking. It shows that you are not free. Right. Now you have to go and check. Are you really not free? Search inside sincerely, if really you are not free. That is the question for you. If you find that you really are not free, then the second question is: Why are you not free? What is making you not free? Find out and tell me. Take your time.

S: [Took a while to respond]

Mahaprabu: Relax. There are no time constraints here. Look deep inside. You have to come out of this problem.

S: I feel like there is no problem now. There is no need to say anything, it feels like. Inside it feels like there is no problem at all.

Mahaprabu: Then no problem. Be inside! Who is calling you out? (Laughing)

S: You.

Mahaprabu: Laughing. Without losing your presence you can answer.

S: There is no urge to say anything. I just want to stay.

Mahaprabu: Yes, you can be or act without losing your presence. See I am here in this state. Nothing affects me. You can also be in this state. It needs practice.

S: That's what you call the state of presence or witnessing?

Mahaprabu: Forget all these things. Words are misguiding us. These teachings are all right, but they are not useful. So don't bring all those terms into your mind. What you really want is a good feeling. And it is not just you who is like that. Everyone wants to feel good.

S: I have a good feeling every day.

Mahaprabu: Then enjoy it. Why do you want to get rid of it and be liberated from that?

S: Because...

Mahaprabu: [Laughing] See the contradiction. When you start with 'because' it shows you are not having a good feeling every day.

S: It is more of a curiosity.

Mahaprabu: Who would want to get rid of a good feeling just for curiosity? [Laughing]

S: It is like an exploration.

Mahaprabu: Who wants to explore? Who is that me? [Now laughing along with the Seeker]

Only if you have a real problem, will you get the answer from me.

S: I don't have a real problem.

Mahaprabu: Then no problem.

S: It is curiosity.

Mahaprabu: If you get awakened, there will be no curiosity about anything. As long as there is curiosity about something, it shows that you are not awakened. (Laughing). Really I want to help you if you need help.

S: It is like I want to explore other layers in me.

Mahaprabu: There is a system. Further layers of this system can be understood only by diving very deep. Curiosity takes you outside usually. You should turn the energy of curiosity inside, towards the system.

S: [Started to say something about discovery etc.]

Mahaprabu: Your toes are moving continuously. Are you aware of that?

S: [Caught by surprise] Yes, I am aware now.

Mahaprabu: If you are in the state of Being you will be aware of that. Once I asked you, you noticed and you are saying you are aware. But it has been moving for some time now.

S: [Again spoke for some time. Mentioned various masters]

Mahaprabu: You need to make a decision to be with a single Master. Once you take that decision, whoever that may be, you need to allocate 3 years to stay with him alone and no one else. If you are not getting what you want after those 3 years, then you have to change your decision. You should not be with them.

S: Why 3 years?

Mahaprabu: So, you can have some experience and feel whether you are free or not. Make a choice. Choose one. Whoever it is. Be with him for 3 years without any expectation, without any concepts about spirituality, just following him. After totally, continuously surrendering him in all aspects for 3 years if you feel you are growing, then you should continue with him. If not change the decision. You have to risk those 3 years.

S: I am 68 years old.

Mahaprabu: No problem. (Pointed at the disciple next to him) 82 years for the body. Another disciple: 75 years. So no problem. Don't worry about the age of the body. As you are not the body, you are not this form. You are something beyond this form. So don't worry. And we should have faith in the Supreme Power, that it will shower its grace on those who are attempting to know themselves. It has the power to extend the life of the body. If you are really a sincere seeker of the Truth, then the universal spirit which is our Mother, will extend the life of the body. Recently we studied here about a Zen Master called Josu. He reached his Master at the age of 60, served him for 20 years and at the age of 80 he was enlightened. After that he served as a Master to all his disciples for 40 more years! So, nature will extend.

Don't worry about the physical age of the body. You are on the right track. Nature has guided you to travel on the right path and my blessing, love and support will always be there for you. Always it will be there. The support from ALL the Brahma Jnanis will be with you; Bhagavan, Annamalai Swami, all of their love and blessings will follow you, because we are travelling in the same path that they travelled. They are our ancestors. They might have dropped the body here but they are not the body. Still their spirit is alive. When you take a few steps towards the Truth, you will touch their heart. Automatically you will receive the Grace. And the difference between them and myself is that they cannot see you as this form. But I can see you as this form. So, you will receive more grace from my side. And definitely you can advance in the path and reach the point where you should actually reach. So, avoid all concepts.

S: Even reaching!

Mahaprabu: No. Let that be there for now. Once you reach, this idea of reaching will also drop by itself. Automatically it will happen. At present you accept it.

January 29th, 2023
Rest House at Paliapattu

Another Seeker Visits

A woman, after having heard about Sri Mahaprabu, visited the Rest house along with her husband. These are always interesting and valuable to watch, the meeting of a person seeing Sri Mahaprabu for the first time.

The husband described how after Girivalam, they went to the temple, where his wife had a near-death like experience where she became very still. Her breath was stopping. She told her husband she was going to die. She could not take a single step. After sometime she came back. The husband gave her water and took her to the hospital. Everything was fine. For the last several years, she had been doing strenuous practices including doing japa (chanting of a mantra) for around 10 hours a day, chanting various shlokas and mantras.

The husband talked about a priest who told her, 'I have been trying for this death experience for 20 years. You are lucky.'

Mahaprabu: The death experience can be created in many ways. In fact, it is going to come anyway to all. For e.g., if a cobra is thrown on your lap it will happen. During Covid, many had diahorrea continuously. The glucose levels drop. A fear of death sets in. So, fear of death is different, death experience is different. She is highly focused on God, loving God, chanting so many mantras, instead of wasting time on so many other things. It shows a good heart. For them, this kind of experience is possible. But what are we going to learn from that experience? After that what? How are we going to grow from that?

Death experience means she will not appear again in this form. One can experience death at the end of life. But she had it in advance, by the Grace of God. So, compared to other human beings, what is she going to do?

Lady: I have stopped chanting mantras. Just don't feel like it. My husband gave me books of Bhagavan but I didn't understand them. Then he got me the book 'Living by the words of Bhagavan', in Telugu (published by the grace of Mahaprabu). That changed me. I understood what Annamalai Swami was telling me. Then I read so many books of Bhagavan. I am chanting Ribhu Gita per the advice of Bhagavan. I have surrendered to Lord Arunachaleshwara totally. I have left it to him. I don't speak with anyone unnecessarily. I have started to see all as God. That too not as form. I want to move to Arunachala and live here. I asked Bhagavan: How do I know myself?

Mahaprabu: Now you are interested in meditation, and not chanting?

L: Yes. Earlier I would do japa for 10 hours a day. Now I don't feel like it. Especially after reading Ribhu Gita I have no interest in japa. I read that, do Puja to the Lord and offer Neivedhyam (a food offering).

M: What is the age of body.

L: 43

M: For this body? (Husband)

H: 54. Sorry for interrupting.

M: Don't worry. You are not disturbing. They (disciples) won't be disturbed. They are practicing internally. If something comes to me to speak, it comes. Otherwise, we meditate. Sometimes we sing songs. Like you, when they came to me, they had all the conversations like you are having. I have heard their experiences, their needs. Now they are in a particular direction towards the destination.

H: She also wants the same thing.

M: Yes. That is why these events are happening. That is why you are both here. So far what you have done may be right, may not be. Maybe helpful. May not be helpful. But from now what to do: You should follow the right path without wasting any more time. The body has a time limit. When the body becomes tired and old, our thinking process, our ability will not help us towards the journey. This is the right time now. Actually, the journey should start at a young age. Say when you want to learn a language, when is ideal? Childhood. Same thing here with meditation. It is already very late. See you are not able to sit for more than an hour. (It was about an hour when Mahaprabu came back out of samadhi. The 2 seekers were sitting on the floor like everyone but were uncomfortable). But look at him. (Dhyanam Swami) He can sit for long. I used to sit for many, many hours on the floor. But now there is a tail bone problem. So, I sit on the bed. I am giving it time to heal. See, Meditation is done here (pointing to the heart). It cannot be done when running. Generally, the body should be made to sit comfortably in the cross-legged position. It gives an attentiveness. In the old days, the teacher would sit under a tree and the children would sit cross-legged on the ground. Sitting in the chair is a relaxed position. It does not lead to that much attentiveness, at least until the point where you are well-trained. Also, with age come other problems. Blood pressure, Arthritis, and so on. So, it is already late.

In the spiritual path, before meeting the Master, the nature, the formless, will guide and show some direction to push us towards a Master who is with form. The formless works through intuition. In that way it moves you to the Master. It is a one-way communication. But with form, it is two-way. Monitoring, observation, communication is all possible. The help of nature is to bring us to a living Master. It hands over. Job over. That is why we say 'Guru Brahma, Guru Vishnu, Guru Devo Maheshwara.' So, a living master's guidelines are very essential to grow from here. Nature sends you to the gate of the school. From there the Master takes over.

H: Even the blessings of other Jnanis like Paramahamsa, Bhagavan will help correct?

M: Yes, their blessings to a deserving soul will guide them towards a living Master. Otherwise, so many in all the ashrams will connect directly with Bhagavan and Paramahamsa and advance towards Realization. But I see them stagnating. Bhagavan is giving them direction to go somewhere, but they are sitting there. If you look at so many religions in the world today, that are based on one person who is equivalent to God. Before that person, that religion did not exist. And after that person, you cannot point at anyone who attained that position. That is a different system. I am talking about the system where there are living Master's available. If you compare these two systems and their followers, you will see that those following a living Master are improving in their lives, growing in character, surrendering and dissolving. But the other system, even after a long time they are still with so many problems, fights and struggles.

Only with a living master, the experience of the beginning is continued. New buds come. Buddha's way of life is still followed. But in the other system there is violence. Similarly, there is a risk in just following a Jnani who is no longer alive. If we just sit and believe that he will take care of everything as he is my God, then we are going into the other system. The followers' lives are likely to be in that mode, and it ends up like the other religions today.

This applies to my case also. Even if this body expires, these disciples with me right now can continue the work. But those who come later and just seeing my photo, sit in front of it, can they have the same progress? One in 100 may. If I were ever to write a book like 'Final Talks', I would say: If you want to still sit here and think I will guide you after my death, you will be mistaken, so please find a living Master. This gate here is open. But the gate you need to go is to a living Master. I have shown these disciples the way and am guiding them step by step. Now they have the maturity about the obstacles and why they have not yet crossed them. The implementation is in their hands. As they are not implementing it, the problem persists. So even if this body (Mahaprabu) goes, they don't need a new Master. They can travel.

Same thing has happened for Buddha, Ramana Bhagavan and myself. In the previous birth, the three of us had Masters. We learned what had to be done in our previous birth. While implementing, the Master lost the body. But that experience is still with us. That experience gained, is not related to the body. Due to karmas the body took birth, we went to school etc. But early on, the questions started arising. Who Am I? Where will the body go after death? That started the quest, and the previous experience stayed, ensuring that we did not need a Master in this birth and yet we attained Realization.

H: Shirdi Sai Baba says even after I leave this body 'My samadhi will guide you.'

M: I was not the follower of Sai Baba. But if I were a follower, I would check. I would ask the devotees if they have experienced and attained. Baba's statement was heard by so many. How many have actually experimented with this? How many actually attained Realization? If they did, then the news would spread. There would be nobody in the ashrams. See, two things are there. Seeking help for worldly affairs or special powers is not what I am talking about. I am talking about Spiritual Growth to the point where your identity dissolves totally.

H: Now I understand.

M: Baba might be right. I have not experimented. One thing I can say. For worldly affairs, you need not even go to a sage or an ashram. Simply having a stone to worship is enough. They go to a stone idol of Muruga in Palani and they come back with their problems solved. They asked for a child and now they have twins. See, at least Baba lived 100 years ago. Muruga? Timeless. If the stone can do it, then definitely a great sage like Baba can help people with their worldly problems. But can they guide you minute by minute in the spiritual journey towards Enlightenment? It is much easier with a living Master.

(Looking at the lady): You have to decide? You have to be very clear. Why do you want meditation? Otherwise, our mind will play games. For example, her sister might wonder. She is chanting 20 lakh times. I need to chant too. Then she will look for a Master. That is how this Girivalam phenonmenon has happened here. In those days, only one or two ants used to go on Girivalam. There was a Tamil movie called Arunachala, Rajnikanth put lights around the Girivalam road. Then this craze started. How? Like you came here. You tell your relatives. They think, 'Oh, she went, we need to go.' The mind makes you want what others have. Now they have started going around mountains in their towns. Businesses are promoting those mountains. Putting a light or fire on top of the mountain during certain times of the year.

Similarly, she should not have in her mind, so many are going for meditation, I also need to. So, one has to be very clear why you want to meditate.

L: Actually, it is not something I am trying to do. I don't want to have another birth.

M: Why don't you want another birth?

L: I don't know. The book says there is no birth and death.

M: You have to find out. It came to you naturally that you don't want another birth. That is well and good. But the question 'Is there birth and death?', you must find out yourself. You must enquire. Just by reading books you are accepting things. I am telling you, don't believe words. You have knowledge. You have enquired about so many things in life. Please do this also as an enquiry. Your intuition is telling you that you should not have another birth. That is great. But give value to your experience. After so many experiences, sorrows, understandings and even tremendous satisfactions, life gave you a feeling, 'I should not have another birth.' Why? The answer is inside you. Find it. Maybe it is due to tremendous satisfaction and the resulting boredom leading to a curiosity. From the first man till now, he has been eating, excreting, having sex, producing children and dying. This is happening till now. Everything else may have changed, but in essence this is what is happening. Imagine the boredom. This may be a reason. Or it may be due to immense suffering.

L: There is no reason.

M: You have to search for the reason. Otherwise, it will be a mere wish. Just like any other wish.

(The lady was hungry. She hadn't eaten from morning).

M: Please give food to the body now, here. See, God never asked us to fast. He only wanted us to run fast towards him. After giving food, I will be here if you want. One thing I will say is don't go behind beliefs. They will take you to all the places that your mind wants to. I want you both of you to advance in your tracks. Don't make sudden decisions. Plan at least 2 days here. Move with these disciples. In 6 months if you come 2 days in a month, that is 12 days and we may have contact also via technology. In these 6 months if both or either of you get convinced, get faith due to your experience, from our talks, the meditation, etc, then this faith is a mature faith. It is taking birth out of your own experience with me. It is yours. That six months will give me enough time also, to see whether I can guide you or not. That time we need to give. It will give us a good communication, communion. We can doubt until that period. We have to doubt! After six months, if your inner feeling says that we can follow Mahaprabu, then you start following. I will never drop you. I will use these six months to observe how sincere you are. Let us give it some time. It is a life. You are going to live a different life. It needs a lot of sincerity and involvement. Not now, but in time it will grow. You can make better decisions. Don't search for new Masters in these six months. In any case you have to stay with one Master for a period of time. It is like going to a doctor for a disease. You stay with him till the time period specified. Then you can think about changing the physician. Go to temples, that is fine. But not for guidelines.

For the disciples here, I say: Initially the communication is through words. But after some time, there is communication without words. So something is going on. They are connected somehow. The message can be communicated without words.

What you are going to get from meditation is an experience of who you are. So far you have been thinking that you are a woman. Based on the body structure. That's why we have male Gods, female Gods and so on. But meditation will show you who you really are. And what is birth, what is death, what is life, what is the real fact about you. It is research. It is not an end. It is a starting point. To know something which cannot be known through the eyes or through the brain. It is not simply being silent. Yes, silence is there, but in that silence, we are going to understand something. We are going to improve our wisdom. When we start understanding the fact about us, so many things start to go away, like fear.

In the mother's uterus this body was there. But how did the life energy enter? The scan shows the physical mass. But how this life entered is not captured in any scan. So many couples are trying but not conceiving. The right cells are there. So, there is something that makes those two cells conceive. We understand everything about the cells through science. But not about how and why the life energy enters. That we can know through meditation. It is a starting point to know about our origin. About who we really are. In this way when you approach it, you will have growth. Otherwise, sitting for silence without understanding, then you will become addicted to it like any other tranquilizer. A mental drug. You will setup a place of solitude. And sit there. The slightest disturbances will frustrate you.

Bhagavan has given us direction on how to enquire and know about ourselves. So, come for 6 months whenever possible.

Mahaprabu gave them fruits, and gave some for their driver too. The devotees thanked Mahaprabu and left.

February 5ᵗʰ, 2023
Rest House at Paliapattu

Satsang with Sri Mahaprabu

May the grace of Bhagavan Ramana Maharshi, Sri Annamalai Swami, Sri Mahaprabu and all the Brahma Jnanis guide you and protect you.

Sri Mahaprabu conducts Satsang regularly in Paliapattu (8 Km from Ramanashramam) during the weekends. Seekers who are very eager to lose their ego and rediscover their true nature are requested to contact us at this link: www.srimahaprabu.org/contact

Please make sure to include your name, contact information, nationality, your present life situation and a detailed background about yourself.

Thank you

www.ingramcontent.com/pod-product-compliance
Lightning Source LLC
Chambersburg PA
CBHW042059150726
48005CB00033B/1204